Essential
Bali
and Jakarta

by

CHRISTINE OSBORNE

Christine Osborne is a travel writer with a
special interest in the East. She has travelled
widely in the Middle East, North Africa and
Southeast Asia. Among the books she has
written is the *Essential Guide to Thailand*, and
her photographs appear in leading
publications.

GW00356808

AA

Produced by the Publishing Division of
The Automobile Association

Written by Christine Osborne
Peace and Quiet section
by Paul Sterry
Consultant: Frank Dawes

Edited, designed and produced by
the Publishing Division of The
Automobile Association. Maps ©
The Automobile Association 1991.

Distributed in the United Kingdom
by the Publishing Division of The
Automobile Association, Fanum
House, Basingstoke, Hampshire,
RG21 2EA

A CIP catalogue record for this book
is available from the British Library.

ISBN 0 7495 0091 3

Published by The Automobile
Association

Typesetting: Microset Graphics Ltd,
Basingstoke
Colour separation: L.C. Repro,
Aldermaston
Printed in Italy by Printers S.R.L.,
Trento

*Front cover picture: Traditional
Dance*

INTRODUCTION TO INDONESIA	4
BACKGROUND TO BALI	9
JAKARTA	17
WHAT TO SEE ON BALI A–Z Gazetteer	37
PEACE AND QUIET Wildlife and Countryside on Bali and Java	77
FOOD AND DRINK	87
SHOPPING	90
ACCOMMODATION	93
CULTURE AND ENTERTAINMENT	94
WEATHER AND WHEN TO GO	100
HOW TO BE A LOCAL	101
PERSONAL PRIORITIES	104
CHILDREN	104
TIGHT BUDGET	105
SPECIAL EVENTS	105
SPORT	107
DIRECTORY	109
LANGUAGE	125
INDEX	127

This book employs a
simple rating system to
help choose which
places to visit:

◆◆◆   do not miss

◆◆   see if you can

◆   worth seeing if
      you have time

INTRODUCTION TO INDONESIA

A green and pleasant land: Indonesia is rich with vegetation

INTRODUCTION TO INDONESIA

Nowhere in the world offers such diverse and fascinating contrasts as the island Republic of Indonesia. Landscape ranges from coral atolls to volcanoes stretching across the backbone of Sumatra, Java, Bali and other islands in the east. Of 300 volcanoes, 128 are active, more than half of which have erupted. More than 300 known ethnic groups, each with its own culture and speaking some 200 distinct languages, inhabit the 13,677 islands in the archipelago. It would take you 38 years of island-hopping to visit each one! Covering a land area of 741,000 square miles (nearly 2 million sq km) the archipelago extends for 3,180 miles (5,120 km), roughly the distance between New York and San Francisco. Astride the equator, Indonesia is covered with lush vegetation – forests, coconut palms and jungle exotica, especially orchids. No fewer

than 15,000 tropical species are recorded. This humid, green habitat is home for many rare animals, including the Java tiger, Komodo dragon and the magnificent birds of paradise (see **Peace and Quiet** pages 77-86).

Indonesia's History

Indonesia's history is like a many-tiered cake with successive migrations and invasions covering the ethnic base. When Hindus from India reached the archipelago about 2,000 years ago, they found an indigenous people, animists (spirit-worshippers), with a distinctive culture. The *Bali Aga*, who still live in separate communities in Bali, are descendants of original inhabitants (see pages 70 and 71).

The first Hindu societies were swallowed up by a powerful Hindu empire, the Sriwijaya, which rose to prominence in southern Sumatra in the 7th century AD and whose influence extended

INTRODUCTION TO INDONESIA

Symbols of two religions, side by side: Jakarta's mosque and cathedral

over much of the Indian Ocean for some 500 years. Buddhism too had reached Indonesia, most impressively represented by the spectacular 8th-century Buddhist temple at Borobodur on Java.

Of great importance in Indonesian history was the 14th-century Hindu kingdom of Majapahit in East Java, under which efforts were made to unify the islands and cultures of Indonesia. Islam was the next invader, largely supplanting Hinduism and Buddhism by the end of the 14th century. European influence began in the 16th century with the arrival of Portuguese traders, later expelled by the British and then the Dutch. The Dutch colonial role began with the establishment of a trading post in Jakarta in 1602. The Japanese occupied Indonesia from 1942 to 1945. Independence was proclaimed in 1945 and eventually recognised by the Netherlands in 1949.

From 1949 to 1965, under President Soekarno, Indonesia's progress was often chaotic and bloody. Thousands were slaughtered following the abortive Communist coup in 1965. Indonesia is now relatively stable under President Suharto, the tough-minded military chief who rose to power after the coup.

Government

Indonesia pursues a form of democratic government based on the philosophy of *Pancasila* (the Five Basic Principles). These are: belief in one God, righteousness and moral humanity, democracy, social justice and unity. The national motto is 'Unity through Diversity'. Central government, the People's Consultative Assembly, determines federal policies from Jakarta. The Assembly appoints the president who holds wide executive powers.

People and Religion

The fifth most densely populated country in the world – about 170 millions – Indonesia is predominantly Muslim. About 87 per cent of people follow orthodox Islam; 7 per cent are Christian; 3 per cent are Hindu or Buddhist and the remaining tribes are animists. About 65 per cent of the total population lives on the island of Java. Jakarta, the Indonesian capital, has a two-thirds Muslim population. The Balinese follow local Balinese-Hinduism. The national language is *Bahasa Indonesia* (Indonesian), but English is understood in most larger towns.

Economy

Despite the growth of tourism and other industries in Bali, village life is still in evidence

Crude oil is Indonesia's major source of foreign exchange. It is the eleventh biggest oil-producer in the world and a member of the OPEC cartel. The economy is based on petroleum exports, agriculture and to an

increasing extent, manufacturing. Farming employs more than half the labour force. Principal crops are foodstuffs for domestic consumption – rice, cassava and corn. Cash crops for export include rubber, coffee and tea. Java and Bali are two of the most intensively cultivated islands in the archipelago. Tourism is only fully exploited on Bali where the west coast resort of Kuta has the highest standard of living in Indonesia. The extension of a tourist industry is Indonesia's greatest potential source of foreign exchange.

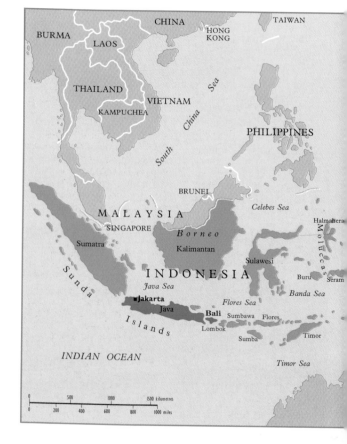

BACKGROUND TO BALI

Writers, artists and travellers have lavished praise on Bali, the jewel-like island planted in the navel of the Indonesian archipelago. Its beautiful women and exotic culture caused many an ancient mariner to jump ship. Although Hindu beliefs reached the island by the 10th–11th centuries, it remained cut off from the outside world until a Dutch invasion in 1906.

A million tourists a year are predicted for Bali by the late 1990s. Despite local hawkers and loud Australians, most newcomers are enchanted by the lush, green isle. People who knew Bali before the tourist boom find many changes but close scrutiny reveals they are superficial. Balinese culture has met Western lifestyle head-on, but instead of being swamped, it has survived.

Behind this miracle are deep religious convictions and close family ties. Balinese beachboys may wear lycra board-shorts and ride Japanese motorbikes, but at heart they are Balinese. Evidence of local resilience is a poignant ceremony each evening in Kuta, the town most affected by tourism. On Bemo Corner – the busiest intersection in Bali – a priest leads prayers amid noise, pollution and curious onlookers.

Somehow the Balinese have managed to master the difficult trick of being 'raped', while retaining their dignity.

Geography and Land-use

Lying eight degrees south of the equator off East Java, Bali is the first in a string of islands known as Nusa Tengarra. It has a land area of 2,170 square miles (5,620 sq km) and measures 87 by 50 miles (140 by 80km): small enough to cycle round.

Central Bali consists of considerable mountain thrusts and active volcanoes. Smoking gently, Gunung Agung – the 'Mother of Mountains' – is 10,306 feet (3,142m). When it erupted

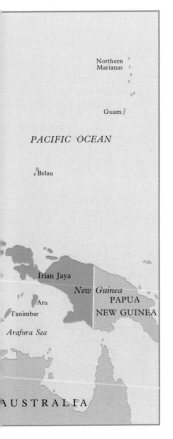

Northern
Marianas

Guam

PACIFIC OCEAN

Belau

Irian Jaya

New Guinea
PAPUA
NEW GUINEA

Aru

Tanimbar

Arafura Sea

AUSTRALIA

in 1963, lava flowed down to the sea with terrible loss of life. Bali's fertile soil and high rainfall make it one of the most productive rice-growing areas in Indonesia. Rising in steps to the sky, the ingeniously irrigated paddy-fields are a masterpiece of ancient engineering. Tabanan and Gianyar are the richest farming areas. There is no special rice-growing season: plants are being sown in one field next to another where rice is being cut. The yield is two, sometimes three crops a year although farming methods remain primitive. Buffalo and cows are used for ploughing, threshing is done by hand. Scarecrows, fluttering ribbons and children playing truant frighten birds away from the ripening grain. Each farm has a small shrine

Seaweed gatherers' haul from the Nusa Lembongan lagoon

where offerings are made to ensure a bountiful harvest. Coffee and exotic fruits are grown on the moist mountain slopes. Copra is important on the coast. There are fledgling shrimp-breeding farms near Negara and Benoa. On the drier north coast cattle are raised for export. Tobacco, kapok and corn are grown and grapes flourish. In the Badung Straits off Klungkung, the island of Nusa Penida is very dry. Occupations are cattle-raising and farming corn and cashew-nuts. The well aerated lagoons off Nusa Lembongan are ideal for seaweed cultivation. Bali teems with fish, but the Balinese are farmers, not fishermen. Painting, sculpting and weaving are important cottage industries. Tourism is a big money-spinner, but most earnings bypass Bali to enrich investors from Jakarta and Surabaya.

History

Bali probably had a Stone Age culture but the earliest records date only from engravings of the 9th century AD. Hindu influence began spreading from Java in the 11th century: the rock-cut tombs of Gunung Kawi in Gianyar district date from this time. The island remained semi-independent until the Pejeng rulers clashed with the Majapahit dynasty (see page 6) in 1343. Gajah Mada, the illustrious Majapahit minister after whom hundreds of Indonesian streets are named, brought the island back under Javanese control. This status quo was maintained during 200 years' rule of the Gelgel dynasty based near present-day Klungkung.

Weakened by the Muslim invasion in the 15th century, the Majapahit dynasty collapsed. There followed a mass exodus of Javanese intelligentsia to Bali – artists, sculptors, scholars and priests taking sacred Hindu texts. Among them was the High Priest Nirartha who introduced new ideas into Bali's already eclectic brand of Hinduism and spirit worship.

Scouring the East Indies for spices, the Dutch reached Bali in 1597. The island was then at the peak of its artistic prosperity, but as it grew rice, not cloves and peppers, the Dutch were not interested and sailed away.

When the Gelgel dynasty began to break up, in the 19th century, Dutch ships reappeared off the outer reefs. Vague salvage rights to a shipwreck were used as a pretext to land Dutch forces on the north coast of Bali. When a second ship foundered off Sanur in 1904, the Dutch demanded damages of 3,000 silver dollars from the Raja of Badung. When he refused to kowtow, they landed and marched on Denpasar. On 20 September 1906, outnumbered but still refusing to surrender, the three princes of Badung led the entire royal family in a ritual *puputan* or mass suicide. Four thousand were killed.

Hearing the news, the kingdoms of Gianyar and Karangasem capitulated. But in Tabanan the raja also committed suicide and the last royal family of Klungkung also opted bravely for a *puputan*. Bali like the rest of Indonesia became part of the Netherlands East Indies.

Dutch rule from Singaraja was low-key as well as short-lived. Bali remained under Japanese occupation throughout World War II and independence for Indonesia was only recognised by The Hague in 1949. Following the attempted coup in 1965, thousands of Communists, including many in Bali, were slaughtered. Today the island makes local decisions at district level, but major policies come from central government in Jakarta.

The People

Bali has a population of around three million. They are generally small-framed people with delicate features and considerable grace. Balinese women are beautiful, fragile creatures with Pepsodent smiles and doe-like eyes. They have always been in demand as foreign brides. Both sexes have a sense of humour, are warm and extremely hospitable towards strangers. Honesty is another trait. Until tourism attracted miscreants from other islands, you could leave things anywhere without risk.

Politeness comes naturally to the Balinese. While doubtless shocked by Western ways, they are too courteous to comment. Extraordinarily creative, they are also deeply religious. Religion and the arts combine in a natural, never-ending pageant.

Religion

Like Islam elsewhere in Muslim Indonesia, Hinduism permeates every aspect of Balinese lives. Balinese-Hinduism is the islanders' own interpretation of ancient Hinduism, an exotic schism involving considerable spirit worship. While much of the culture is based on the main Hindu deities – Vishnu, Shiva and Brahma – the Balinese have their own gods: Sun-Gods, Moon-Gods, Turtle Gods and scores of other mythical creatures. Evil spirits inhabit the sea. The Balinese are terrified of going out too far and few can swim. Instead they worship the mountains believed to be the dwelling places of the gods. And the gods and spirits must constantly be appeased. As well as in the temples, every house has a shrine where offerings are made of small palm-leaf baskets containing flowers, rice, salt, chilli and burning incense. Balinese-Hinduism is directed at maintaining a balance between opposing forces: good and evil,

hot and cold, etc. Harmony is essential. People are, however, exceptionally superstitious and in reality, spirits dominate their psyche. Nothing important is arranged without consulting a priest who determines the most auspicious date.

Temples

Bali has more temples, or *pura,* than anywhere in the world. Every village has several and an estimate of the total might be 20,000. *Pura* is Sanskrit, meaning a space surrounded by a wall. Each *pura* is aligned towards the mountains; the holiest shrines are found at this end of the courtyard. The most important temple, the *pura puseh,* is dedicated to the village founders; *pura desa,* in the centre of the village, is for spirits protecting the people in everyday life. In the direction of the sea is the *pura dalem,* or Temple of the Dead.

Temples are basically similar. They consist of multiple courtyards entered through an elaborate gateway flanked by fearsome guardians. The outer courtyard with the alarm drum, or *kulkul,* is used for meetings. It is also used for preparing food on the occasion of a festival. The inner courtyard is likewise entered through a narrow gate up a flight of steps also guarded by mythical creatures or small, protective shrines. Inside are the tall, multi-roofed towers, or *merus,* and smaller stone shrines dedicated to various gods. An important temple has a throne associated with Surya, the Balinese Sun-God. A soaring

Gifts of fruit are taken as offerings for temple celebrations

piece of sculpture, it depicts the world's three cosmic levels. Serpents, turtles and *garudas* – winged bird-men – are among an elaborate assemblage of creatures. Balinese have no objection to your visiting their temples, but custom decrees you wear a sash (see page 103). A temple is a quiet place until the occasion of its *odalan*, or 'birthday'. Every temple celebrates this feast in honour of its consecration once every 210 days on the Balinese calendar. *Odalan* is greatly anticipated by the villagers and prayers, feasting and entertainment last for three days, a rare occasion to stay up late.

A procession with women bearing vast pyramids of fruit, cakes and flowers on their heads is one of the sights of Bali, as they proudly walk like mannequins, in single file to the temple. Inside, their offerings are blessed by the priest sprinkling holy water on them. They are placed in a row as part of the general decoration and the women dance the slow *pendet*. Enlivened by the music of a *gamelan* (see page 94-5), this scene in the sacred innermost courtyard may not be accessible to visitors. In the temple precincts, however, are shadow-plays, dance-dramas, foodstalls and probably a cockfight. The Balinese are very gracious about tourists attending a temple festival but do not be too pushy and do not use a camera flash.

With so many temples, it is not hard to find one having a festival. So colourful a spectacle is it, that the Bali Government Tourism Office publishes a special calendar. Also including other important holidays, it may be obtained free from their offices (see **Directory** page 123).

Cremation

The elaborate ceremony
surrounding a cremation has
become a tourist attraction.
Indeed, you can have a
'cremation tour' — the genuine
event. Some tourists are
surprised at the jubilation, but a
local funeral is a happy
occasion. There are no tears
when someone dies on Bali.
The Balinese believe a person
consists of three bodies:
physical, cerebral and spiritual.
The body is the temple of the
soul and only when it is
destroyed is the cycle
complete. It is a sacred duty
falling on every Balinese to give
the soul of a parent, or relative,
a suitable send-off.

A poor family may keep a
corpse for years until they can
afford a proper funeral. It is
buried in a coffin and the fluids

*To baffle the soul of the dead, a
funeral bier is spun in circles*

drained off to prevent
decomposition. When a high-
caste person dies, and is to be
cremated, the 'poor body' is
then exhumed to participate in
the funeral of the wealthy
person. When a surviving
member of the royal family died
recently, some 500 corpses
were cremated at the same
time. A Brahman priest, on the
other hand, may not be buried
and he is cremated quickly.
Aware of the cost involved, a
rich man saves for his cremation
— and it is expensive. Costs
include the priest's fee, food
and entertainment as well as a
bill for the ornate ceremonial
towers and sarcophagi built by
village artisans.

When the family can afford it,
they retrieve the remains of
their relative on a date set by
the priest. Covered with white
cloths, the corpse is placed on a
decorated bier outside the
house. Ritual accessories are

laid on the platform. Among these are a rice-filled coconut, symbolising the heart, and a small eggshell lamp representing the soul. Important rites revolve around two effigies of the soul: one a silhouette made from a palm-leaf, the other made from a thin tablet of sandalwood. The deceased's name is attached to each effigy, or *adegam*.

On the eve of the cremation, huge quantities of food arrive. Men sit up all night preparing rice, *lawar* (raw meat and blood) and other dishes for the feast, shared between hundreds. On the great day, women dress in their best including a black headscarf. Commercialism being what it is on Bali, a rich household may provide black T-shirts for male mourners and members of the *gamelan*. Then what seems a sober ceremony explodes to life.

Urged on by the *gamelan*, dozens of men rush to transport the corpse to the cremation site. Jogging through the rice-paddies, the procession is one of the most fantastic sights in Southeast Asia. It is led by women carrying offerings. Bearers follow with huge cremation towers, 8-10 tiers high, made of bamboo, tinsel, cloth, mirrors and flowers. There may be as many as 50 to 80 if the deceased was a Brahman. In the middle, on a richly gilded bier, rides the corpse. A priest hangs on, half-way up the tower, throwing holy water over the crowd. An enormous effigy of Bhoma – Son of the Earth – wild, winged and displaying huge fangs, covers the base of each tower. Every 50 metres, the procession halts, and bearers carrying the corpse spin around wildly with the priest hanging on grimly. The method in this apparent madness is to confuse the soul so that it cannot find its way back to the house. Round and round it is spun on the men's shoulders. Laughing and falling over, they all try to lend a hand to show loyalty to the deceased. Huge sarcophagi are also carried to the cremation site. Caste (see page 103) dictates their shape: a white bull (or cow) for a Brahman, a winged lion for a Satria, and a mythical creature, half-elephant, half-fish, for a Sudra. At the cremation site, these are placed above the corpse under a canopy of white cloth. Immediate relatives slash the shrouds exposing the corpse. Reciting final prayers, the priest smashes pots of holy water on the ground around the funeral pyre. The *adegams* are placed on the chest and old Chinese coins are scattered over the body (symbolic of a ransom to Yama, a deity of death).

The tower, sarcophagus and pavilion are now set alight. As matches are considered unclean, a blow torch is used on the skull and feet. Everyone watches the tower collapse as smoke billows. When the deceased has burned, a new procession forms to take the ashes to the sea.

Piodalan, a final cleansing of the soul, occurs several months later when more offerings are cast into the sea.

JAKARTA

A Rewarding Stop-over
Muslim Jakarta, the big,
sprawling capital of Indonesia,
is a different world from rural
Bali. However, it is a fascinating
place to stop off *en route* to Bali
to experience another aspect of
the varied land that is
Indonesia.

Introduction
Jakarta has an unsalubrious
reputation which deters tourism.
There is no denying that it is hot
(with 95 per cent humidity
November – April), crowded
(more than 8 million inhabitants),
polluted (you grow old waiting
in the traffic-jams) and parts of it
stink.
On the plus side, Jakarta has
excellent cheap food and a
nightlife second to none. It
abounds in marvellous, musty
old museums and there are
streets of antiques and
handicrafts from all over the
archipelago. Utara (north)
Jakarta in particular has many
curiosities from Old Batavia, (as
Jakarta used to be called), and
the harbour, filled with
tall-masted *Bugis* schooners, has
little changed in 500 years.
This is the tourist face of Jakarta.
Downtown is a busy, modern
business area of de luxe hotels,
department stores and an
estimated 400 banks. Covering
240 square miles (630 sq km),
the city is roughly divided into:
Utara Jakarta – Pelabuhan Sunda
Kelapa (harbour) area and Old
Batavia/Chinatown; Selatan
(south) Jakarta – satellite city,
higher income area: Timur
(east) Jakarta – housing estates:

and Barat (west) Jakarta – largely a trade and consumer goods district.

Known as the 'Mother City' – *Ibn Kota* – Jakarta is the centre of government, commerce and industry. It is also the film, fashion and literacy centre – all the papers are printed here – and although Bali claims more tourists, it remains the main gateway to Indonesia.

History

Jakarta began life as a small trading port at the mouth of the Ciliwung river, today the **Kali Besar** area. In 1527 it was named 'Jayakarta' (Glorious Victory) by Fatahillah, a conquering Muslim prince who ousted the Hindu rajas (local Hindu inscriptions date from AD5).

In the early 1600s, a Dutch East India fleet established a trading post in 'Jayakarta'. Renaming it 'Batavia' (after a German tribe who once occupied the Dutch lowlands), they built a new town. Almost like a 'tropical Amsterdam', it had intersecting canals, a market square, *stadhuis* (town hall) and houses with red-tiled roofs.

Administrative buildings were constructed around a huge, grassy *padang*, now Medan Merdeka, or Merdeka Square. But because of its terrible climate, it was unsuitable for Europeans: more Dutch are said to have died there than in any other colony in Asia.

Much of Jakarta's post-1700s architecture has survived. Fatahillah Square (Taman Fatahillah), in particular, is a fascinating window on Old Batavia. Unfortunately, just as many elegant old Chinese residences have been demolished to make way for city planning. The plethora of city monuments – to the army, athletes and heroes – was built during the Soekarno era. Development has continued under President Suharto.

The city's layout is hard to sort out, but once you know your way about in relation to Jalan MH Thamrin, the long, traffic-congested, central artery, Jakarta is relatively well planned. Construction continues unabated; some of the most important buildings (Grand Hyatt, Kartika Plaza, Sahid Jaya hotels, etc) are owned by the Suharto family. The word 'Jaya' after many names means 'success' in *Bahasa Indonesia* (the national language). Warts and all, Jakarta is a success story and the absence of hasslers is a big advantage when shopping and sightseeing (but watch out for pickpockets!).

Sightseeing

Jakarta is full of interesting old treasures, but because sights are scattered over the city, you need time and patience. Certain parts can be seen on foot, or by taxi, but you are urged to take a City Tour. A guide who knows his way about greatly simplifies sightseeing. Comprehensive coach tours lasting five to six hours are operated daily by Panorama Tours and Setia Tours and Travel, with hotel pick-up. Apexindo Express Tours and Travel Services arrange excellent tailor-made visits of Jakarta and elsewhere. Or

consult your hotel travel agency.
Apexindo Express, Office
49-50-51, 3rd floor, east wing
arcade, Borobodur Inter-
Continental Hotel (tel:
376598-376524).
Panorama Tours, Jalan Balik
Papan 22B, Jakarta Pusat
(tel: 350438-376718).
**Setia Tours and Travel
(Grayline),** Jalan Pinangsia Raya,
Glodok Plaza Block B No 1
(tel: 6390008-6492898).

WHAT TO SEE

◆◆
GLODOK
area of Jalan Pintu Besar
This is the heart of 'old
Chinatown' with Chinese
temples and houses in back
streets off the busy commercial
centre. The temple complex
known as the 'Temple of Golden
Virtue', dating from the mid-17th
century, is the focal point of the
Chinese community. Explore on
foot, daytime only. A good
shopping and eating area.

◆◆
ISTIQLAL MOSQUE
Medan Merdeka
Planted opposite the cathedral
and overlooked by the
Borobodur Inter-Continental
hotel, this is Southeast Asia's
biggest mosque, built by
President Soekarno. English-
speaking conducted tours are
recommended if you have
never been inside a mosque.
Women must cover their heads
with a scarf and all must discard
shoes outside. Photography is
permitted. *Closed:* Friday
morning.

*Jakarta, where most of the people
are Muslim, has the biggest mosque
in Southeast Asia*

◆◆
MEDAN MERDEKA
'Freedom Square' is one of the
largest public squares in the
world. In the centre, the lofty
National Monument occupies
the geographical heart of
Jakarta. Once a military parade
ground, the huge park has been
surrounded by state
bureaucratic headquarters since
Dutch times. To the north are
the **Istana Negara** (State Palace)
and **Istana Merdeka** (Freedom
Palace). The modern parliament
building is also on the square as
is the National Museum (see
page 23), together with several
banks and hotels.

The soaring National Monument: the
symbol of Indonesian independence

◆◆
MONUMEN NASIONAL (NATIONAL MONUMENT)
Medan Merdeka
Known as MONAS, the marble
obelisk is 450 feet (137m) high.
It symbolises Indonesia's
independence struggle against
the Dutch. Take the lift up
(entrance charge) for a great
view, and go early, before the
coachloads of Japanese tourists
arrive.
There is a small museum
beneath the monument,
presenting Indonesia's history
through a series of dioramas.
In the Independence Hall, you
can listen to the voice of
Soekarno broadcasting the
Declaration of Independence.
Open: daily 08.00 – 17.00 hrs.
WC available.

◆◆◆
PASAR IKAN
harbour area
Traffic is so bad around Taman
Fatahillah, the main square of
old Dutch Batavia, that it can be
quicker to walk to **Pelabuhan
Sunda Kelapa,** popularly known
as **Pasar Ikan,** or fish market.
The name is slightly misleading;
a fish market, or auction, is held
here at 03.00 hours and by 09.00
hours all you have is the smell.
Shops sell dehydrated turtles,
lobsters, shells and coral. Walk
down past the old, cream
warehouses towards the
harbour. In tiny, fetid alleys
shops sell nautical and fishing
equipment. You may be the only
tourist, but you will meet others
on the long harbourfront lined
with *Bugis* sailing vessels. Sunda
Kelapa is still one of the most
important port-calls in the

Orchids create a blaze of colour in the Taman Anggrek Jakarta

archipelago. If you ask courteously, most sailors do not mind you coming on board to look around. Up to 100 feet (30m) long, the great sailing vessels are made in Kalimantan and South Sulawesi. Hawkers sell miniature boats and other marine artefacts. Now a putrid canal, the Ciliwung river opening into the bay was a vital means of transport inland in the 15th century. Other vestiges of Dutch dominion in Indonesia are shipyards and a 17th-century watch tower, **Gedung Syahbandar** (Harbourmaster's Office). For a small fee you can climb to the top of the tower and have a fine view of the port area. You look down on to two 16th-century warehouses forming the **Museum Bahari** (see **Museums** page 22). Wear old shoes to visit the harbour area. Avoid midday. There is a small

charge for entry to the wharf area, payable at the toll-gate.

◆◆
TAMAN ANGGREK GELORA SENAYAN
(ORCHID GARDEN)
Indonesia is well known for orchids and Taman Anggrek, situated in the Senayan Sports Complex, is a commercial orchid park open to the public. There are 100 species and orchid auctions are held at 02.00-03.00 hrs.
Open: daily from 09.00 hrs. Admission charge.
Other orchid parks are at Jalan Parman-Slip and **Taman Mini Indonesia** (see **Excursions** page 24).

◆◆◆
TAMAN FATAHILLAH
Old Batavia (or Kota)
This large, paved square overlooked by Jakarta City Museum (the former *stadhuis*) was the main square in Dutch Batavia. Markets were held

here and criminals punished, and early residents used to fetch water from the central well. Note the 16th-century Portuguese cannon (popularly called *Si Jagur* – 'Mr Sturdy') on the north side of the square. Its clenched fist symbol was believed to cure infertility – barren women used to sit astride the cannon and offer flowers. The present cannon was recast from an earlier one. Today a busy 'flea market' is held around it. The 'Restaurant' Fatahillah, an attractive old building on the corner, offers dusty images of Dutch café-society in bygone days, along with refreshments, *objets d'art* and a dirty WC.

Take your time in the vicinity of Fatahillah Square as there is much to see and enjoy, including the **Museum Fatahillah, Museum Seni Rupa** and **Museum Wayang** (City, Fine Arts and Puppet Museums – see **Museums** pages 23–24).

◆

TAMAN IMPIAN JAYA ANCOL (ANCOL DREAMLAND)

This is a huge, open-air recreational park and crafts centre on Jakarta Bay. Basically for local families, it has the Disney-inspired **Dunia Fantasi,** including a swimming-pool, water-slides, oceanarium with performing dolphins, sealions and penguins, bowling complex, *warung* (food-stalls) and drive-in theatre. There is also cottage accommodation and an 18-hole golf course. Excellent for children, but crowded at weekends.

Open: daily. Admission charge.

Artists at work in the local leisure spot Taman Impian Jaya Ancol

Museums

Jakarta has many fascinating museums. The usual opening hours are Tuesday to Thursday 09.00-14.00 hrs; Friday to 11.00 hrs; Saturday to 13.00 hrs; Sunday to 15.00 hrs. Closed Monday. Entry charge, with extra for a camera.

◆◆◆

MUSEUM BAHARI

near Pelabuhan Sunda Kelapa
This Marine Museum is in two restored 16th-century warehouses used by the Dutch East India Company to store tea, coffee, cloth, spices and other valuable exports from Java. One building exhibits trade memorabilia, the other deals with maritime history. There are some good model boats.

◆◆◆
MUSEUM PUSAT
(NATIONAL MUSEUM)
Jalan Merdeka Barat 12,
Medan Merdeka
Built in the 18th century by the
Batavian Society for Arts and
Sciences, it houses the world's
biggest exhibition of
'Indonesiana', with a huge
collection of Oriental ceramics,
models of traditional buildings
and *prahu* (native sailing ships).
See also the huge ethnic map
representing many of
Indonesia's different tribes,
showing that in prehistoric
times, Indonesia was connected
by a land bridge to the Asian
mainland. Bronzes are on the
second floor, the Gold Room is
only open on Sunday: highlights
are the *kris* (daggers), handles
studded with precious stones.
Open: as given on page 22,
except opens 08.30 hrs Tuesday
to Thursday. For information
tel: 360976.

◆◆◆
MUSEUM FATAHILLAH
(CITY MUSEUM)
Taman Fatahillah
Built in 1627, the museum was
formerly the *stadhuis*, or town
hall, in Old Batavia. Rather dark
and musty, the two-storey
building oozes history – and
suffering. Basements in the
wings were the infamous 'water
prisons' where prisoners were
incarcerated in flooded cells.
Note the window bars outside
along Jalan Pintu Besar. Exhibits
in the museum include Oriental
and Dutch porcelain, coins,
weapons and antique furniture.
There are also portraits of
former governor-generals,
native princes and national
heroes, plus displays of ancient
maps.
Open: as given on page 22. For
information tel: 67901.

◆◆
MUSEUM SENI RUPA JAKARTA
(FINE ARTS)
Jalan Taman Fatahillah 2
Housed in the old courts of
justice, built in classic
19th-century Dutch colonial
architectural style, the museum
contains numerous art
collections by Indonesia's finest
painters, from the Raden Saleh
era to contemporary times.
There is also a ceramics
museum (**Museum Keramik**).
Descriptions are mainly in
Indonesian. See in conjunction
with the City and Puppet
Museums.
All open: daily 09.00-14.00 hrs.
(For information tel: 676090).

MUSEUM TEKSTIL
(TEXTILE MUSEUM)
Jalan Satsuit Tuban 4
A display of handwoven textiles
from all over Indonesia is housed
in an ornate, 19th-century house.
A visit is essential if you want to
buy fabrics. Every *batik* centre
is represented with an entire
room devoted to *ikat* (double-
weaving). There are also rare
textiles from remote islands in
the archipelago. The museum is
located in southwest Jakarta.
Open: Tuesday to Sunday
09.00-14.00 hrs. For information
tel: 365367.

MUSEUM WAYANG
(PUPPET MUSEUM)
Jalan Pintu Besar Utara 27
Housed in a former church, the
museum exhibits *wayang*
(shadow puppets) and dolls –
both highly developed art-forms
in Indonesia. There is also
puppetry from other Asian
countries. Performances take
place in the rear of the museum
every alternate Sunday
morning. Photography is
permitted at a charge.
Open: usual times (see page 22)
except closes 14.00 hrs Sunday.
For information tel: 679560.

Other 'special interest' museums
are: **Museum Perangko** (stamps);
Museum Abri Satria Mandala
(armed forces), Jalan Gatot
Subroto (opposite the Kartika
Chandra Hotel); **Gedung Arsip
Nasional Museum,** (national
archives), Jalan Gajahmada 111;
Museum Puri Bhrakti Renatama
(Presidential, with a collection
of state gifts).

Churches
Driving about Jakarta, you will
pass several interesting old
churches, including:
St Mary's Kathedral, Jalan
Kathedral 7. On the north side of
Benteng Square facing the
newer Istiqlal Mosque, it is
19th-century, restored
(Catholic).
Gereja Immanuel, Jalan
Merdeka Timur 10, east side of
Merdeka Square. Dutch
Protestant built in the 1830s, it
has an English service, Sunday
17.00 hrs.
Sion Church: Jalan Pangeran
Jayakarta 1, near Fatahillah
Square. Built in the late 17th
century for the Portuguese
community in Old Batavia.
Known as the 'Portuguese
Church', it is Jakarta's oldest.
View the interior Tuesday to
Saturday, 09.00-15.00 hrs.

Excursions

TAMAN MINI INDONESIA
(BEAUTIFUL INDONESIA IN
MINIATURE)
*7½ miles (12km) south of city
centre*
Indonesia's answer to
Disneyland is the most popular
trip to make from Jakarta.
A huge open-air cultural and
amusement park, it covers 295
acres (120 hectares). From the
city it is a 30- to 60-minute drive,
depending on the traffic.
Pavilions built in traditional
styles act as a window on the
customs and lifestyles of
Indonesia's 27 provinces. The
complex features a museum,
theatre, bird park, orchid
garden, miniature train rides,
open-sided trams, cable cars

and boating. It surrounds a man-made lake, landscaped to represent the archipelago. Obtain a programme to see what's on; there are special Cultural Shows on Sunday. Near the entrance is the **Indonesia Museum** built in traditional Balinese-style architecture. It is the best displayed museum in Indonesia. On the ground floor is a spectacular exhibition of national dress and wedding costumes from every region. Other displays include a Balinese tooth-filing ceremony and hunting implements from Timor (1st floor) and traditional weaving tools, superb *ikat* textiles and silverware from east Java and Bali (3rd floor). Look up at the superbly carved roof depicting a lotus flower: central Javanese craftwork. Do not miss the sculpture of a man and his fighting cock carved from a single pice of *johar* wood which took Igusti Mede Bawa, Indonesia's most famous

wood-carver two years to sculpt. Photography is forbidden.

Within Taman Mini is a huge **Bird Park** with over 500 native species and one Spanish flamingo in spacious walk-through aviaries. Do not miss the birds of paradise, hornbills, and crested pigeons. The stream represents the Wallace line, symbolically dividing the birds inhabiting eastern and western zones.

Clean WCs available.

Taman Mini is clean and well laid-out. You will need a day to see it thoroughly. Miss the shops, but eat at the *warung* (food-stalls). Avoid at weekends.

Open: 09.00-16.00 hrs daily. Entry charge with extra fees for cable car rides, tours by ox-cart and the swimming pool.

Crested pigeons, with their luminous blue plumage, are among Taman Mini's beautiful birds

Several tour operators include Taman Mini in a daily tour. Independent travellers take bus 408 from outside Sarinah Department Store, Jalan MH Thamrin, to Cilitan Terminal. Then catch red mini-bus no 2, marked TMII. Allow one hour. Do not consider Taman Mini is only for children; it is highly recommended to adults.

Other excursions, for shorter or longer stays are:

◆◆
KEBUN BINATANG RAGUNAN (RAGUNAN ZOO)
Jalan Ragunan, Pasar Minggu area
About nine miles (15km) from the city, this small, but interesting collection, kept in habitat enclosures rather than cages, includes Komodo dragons, dwarf buffalo, pygmy monkeys and orang-utans. There are also native birds and lizards. The botanical garden is worth a visit.
Open: daily 08.00 – 18.00hrs.
Avoid at weekends.
Amenities include food-stalls, shade and WCs.

◆
LUBANG BUAYA
10 miles (16km) southeast of Jakarta
Tours visit this massive monument *en route* to Taman Mini Indonesia. It commemorates the murder of seven Indonesian generals killed in the Communist coup of 30 September 1965. Their mutilated corpses were stuffed down the well, or *lubang*.
Thought-provoking.
Entry charge.

◆◆◆
PULAU SERIBU (THOUSAND ISLANDS)
Pulau Seribu comprises 118 tropical islands dotted across the vast expanse of Jakarta Bay. It has better beaches than Bali, but the islands suffer from a lack of publicity. Day-trips are available, but when you reach the islands – Seba, Putri or Pelangi – you will wish to spend the night ... and the next ... The only let-down is the poor cooking, but catch your own fish and they will cook it. Only seven of the islands are inhabited, by fishermen whose nets you pass on the boat trip. All are ringed by coral with good skin-diving off the beach, or scuba-diving from a wooden *prahu*. The entire area is a National Marine Park and home to many birds and also *biawaks*, a smaller cousin (one metre long) of the Komodo dragon.
The climate is tropical with average temperature 32°C (90°F). Best months are April to September – August is crowded. Casual beachwear is worn day and evenings. A dive-shop hires out equipment and you can buy a diving package with an Indonesian companion. Take gear if you plan to fish.
Three islands are packaged by Biltour Cruise Division, ground floor lobby, Hyatt Aryaduta, Jalan Prapatan, Jakarta.
Pelangi. 32 acres (13 hectares), 50 miles (80km) from Jakarta. White sand beach, tropical growth, 29 large, comfortable, air-conditioned cottages with hot shower, 220V electricity, radio. Meals in attractive restaurant and a natural

*Pulau Seribu (Thousand Islands) –
a desert island fantasy come true*

aquarium in the reef. Licensed.
Visited by overseas cruise
ships. Moderately expensive.
Putri. Ten minutes by *prahu*
from Pelangi. 17 acres (7
hectares) with 31 air-
conditioned cottages in lovely
surroundings. Fishing and diving
available. A resident doctor is
shared with Pelangi and Seba.
Moderately expensive.
Seba. Lying opposite Putri. Ten
acres (4 hectares) and, like the
other islands, traffic-free. There
are no shops or police. 25 basic,
clean, comfortable bungalows
under palms and she-oaks. The
bar-restaurant with 'muzak' and
TV needs a good chef. Ideal for
nature-lovers with a natural
island aquarium containing fish
and small sharks; turtle-breeding

programme; birds and *biawaks*.
Moderate.

There are daily departures from
Ancol Dreamland marina by
speedboat. Ferries take nearly
four hours. Daily charter flights
from Halim airport to Pulau
Panjang take 25 minutes. From
here there is a ferry on to Pulau
Putri.

PRACTICALITIES

Accommodation
The location of your hotel is the
key to sightseeing in Jakarta. It
is also advisable to pay more than
usual for safe, comfortable
accommodation. Cheaper
establishments are often noisy
and dirty. Backpacker-type
losmen (rooms to let) along Jalan
Jaksa attract various
undesirables.

Luxury Class
Borobodur Inter-Continental,
Jalan Lapangan Banteng
Selatan, Jakarta 10710 (tel:
370108). Large hotel with
attractive décor, huge lobby
with shops and Apexindo Travel
Agency. Near the central
Mosque and 15 minutes by taxi
from the commercial area.
Jakarta Hilton, Jalan Jendral
Gatot Subroto, Senayan, Jakarta
10002 (tel: 583051). The 664
tastefully decorated rooms
overlook lush tropical gardens.
Located 10 minutes by taxi to
central Jakarta and includes
restaurants, shopping plaza,
large swimming pool, nine

*Poolside luxury is provided at the
Hyatt Aryaduta in Jakarta*

tennis courts and three squash
courts. Highly recommended to
business travellers. There is a
'Lady Hilton' check-in and
private floor for women guests.
Hyatt Aryaduta, Jalan Prapatan
44-48, Jakarta 10110. Hotel with
340 rooms in one of the best
locations in Jakarta, only 35
minutes from the airport, 10
minutes by taxi to the banking
district, and within walking
distance of the good shopping
area, National Monument and
museums. Rear rooms have a
view of the river. Regency VIP
service available. Good choice
of restaurants. Excellent
security. Business centre.
Grand Hyatt. Due to open 1991
with 450 de luxe rooms in
central Jakarta.

First Class
Hotel Indonesia, Jalan MH
Thamrin, Jakarta 10310 (tel:
320008). Good-value
government-owned hotel, after
recent extensive renovation. Just
10 minutes' walk to Sarinah
Department Store and five
minutes by taxi to the
commercial area, banks,
offices, etc.
President, Jalan MH Thamrin 59,
Jakarta 10350 (tel: 320508).
Owned by JAL (Japanese
Airlines), it receives mainly
Japanese guests. Good location.
Sari Pacific, Jalan MH Thamrin,
Jakarta (tel: 323707). Also on
Jakarta's main road near banks
and shops. Average rooms.

Tourist Class
Hotel Menteng I, Jalan
Gondangdia Lama 28 (tel:
325208). Has 150 pleasant rooms;
check first as some are airless.
Small pool, friendly atmosphere.

Hotel Menteng II, Jalan Cikini Raya 105 (tel: 325543). Pleasant for what it offers. In a busy area and with a tiny pool. Poor foreign exchange rate at both Menteng hotels.

Marco Polo, Jalan Cik Ditoro (tel: 325409). Near Jalan Surabaya 'antiques street' and with 181 reasonable rooms. Popular with Japanese groups. Overseas calls must be paid for in cash. Good value.

Putri Duyung Cottages, Taman Impian Jaya Ancol (tel: 680108). Individual cottages on Jakarta Bay, popular with executives using Ancol golf course. Also excellent for families – kitchens, video programmes, water-slides and oceanarium in Ancol. Central Jakarta is 30-50 minutes by taxi. Good value, but isolated for an independent traveller.

Sabang Hotel, Jalan Agus Salim (tel: 354301). Pleasant, medium-sized hotel. Excellent location near shops and restaurants. Small pool, homely atmosphere. Ideal for couples and independent travellers. 30 minutes from airport.

Wisata International, Jalan MH Thamrin (tel: 320308). In the city centre near Grand Hyatt. Good value, but no atmosphere.

Economy

Hotel Pasarbaru, Jalan Pasar Baru Selatan 6 (tel: 366474). Small, clean, modern hotel in busy Pasar Baru (night market area). Recommended to budget travellers. Ask for rear room.

Karya Hotel, Jalan Jaksa 32-34 (tel: 320484). The most expensive in a range of backpacker-type *losmen* on Jalan Jaksa – 15 minutes' walk to the city centre. Cheap enough, but not clean enough.

Transaera Hotel, Jalan Merdeka Timur 16 (tel: 351373). Old-style hotel set back on a busy road. Near shops and National Monument. Comfortable, though drab rooms. Indonesian food only.

Wisma Ise, Jalan Wahid Hasyim 168 (tel: 333463). 20 quiet rooms located off Jalan MH Thamrin, Jakarta's main thoroughfare.

Nightlife and Entertainment

Jakarta's nightlife is the best kept secret in Asia. It ranges from select cocktail music to swinging *karaoke* bars, discos and cabaret. Sleaze is inconspicuous. The biggest concentration of nightspots is in Chinatown.

Hotel Lounge Bars with Music

The following are recommended: **Ambassador Lounge** (Hyatt Aryaduta), **Kudus Bar** (Hilton), **Ramayana Lounge** (Indonesia), **Clipper Lounge and Club Bar** (Oriental), **Lobby Bar and Ria Lounge** (Sahid Jaya), **Pendopo Lounge/Bar** (Borobodur Inter-Continental), **Kattleya Bar** (President).

Pub Crawls

Most bars open from noon until around 02.00 hours. 'Happy hours' offer discounted drinks between 17.00 and 20.00 hours. Drinking holes range from rough to élite. Measures are generous. All bars have a décor theme with live entertainment likely to be Filipino. The **'Tavern at the Hyatt'**, a combo of pub and *Bierkeller*, is popular. Also suggested: **After 8, Jaya Pub, Amigos, Rumours, Topaz.**

A huge number of massage bars/discos are found on Jalan Mangga Besar in Chinatown; they include **Valentino, Fairy Garden, Our Place,** etc. *Karaoke* bars are the rage: **OK! Karaoke 2** is recommended (18.00-0.400 hours).

Discos
Jakarta boasts the biggest discos in Asia. The **Regent Space Palace** holds 4,000. Equally popular are **Dynasty** and **Stardust** in the Jakarta Towers Hotel, Chinatown. Stardust is a good bet. Cover includes beer, or soft drink.

Night-clubs/Cabaret
Nirwana Supper Club (Hotel Indonesia). Dinner, western cabaret, city views.
Blue Ocean Restaurant and Nite Club, Jalan Hayam Wuruk 5. Bright, crowded, choice of 300 hostesses.
LCC Nite Club, opposite the National Monument.
Sky Room Restaurant and Nite Club, Duta Merlin Shopping Centre, Chinatown.
Shamrock, Ancol Dreamland.

Evening Tours
There is a choice of several tours. **Jakarta After Dark** (minimum of two persons) is operated by Panorama nightly. Four hours' duration. Includes dinner, cultural performance and disco. **Grayline Night-Club** tour includes oriental cabaret and night-club. Five hours' duration; tour fare includes dinner and a drink.

Indonesian Cultural Performances
For *Wayang Orang* and *Ketoprak* (Javanese dance dramas) performances visit Bhatara Theatre at Jalan Kalilio. *Wayang Orang* is staged nightly from 20.15 to midnight except on Monday and Thursday nights.
Wayang Kulit (shadow puppet plays) and *Wayang Golek* (three-dimensional puppet shows) are staged alternately at the National Museum, Jalan Merdeka Barat on Sunday evenings starting at 20.00 hours. At the Wayang Museum the play begins at 10.00 hrs on Sunday mornings.
The *Srimulat Show* is a popular Javanese comedy show, staged nightly from 20.00 – 23.00 hrs at Taman Ria Senayan.
The *Miss Tjitjih Show* is a Sundanese Folk Drama from West Java, staged nightly at Jalan Kabel Pendek, Cempaka Baru at 19.00 hrs and 21.00 hrs. Several pavilions at Taman Mini Indonesia present various traditional dances on Sundays and holidays from 10.00–14.00 hrs, and local dramas are put on on the open stage at Ancol Dreamland.
Traditional performances are also staged at TIM (Taman Ismail Marzuki), the Jakarta arts centre, at Jalan Cikini Raya 73. Its monthly programme is available in hotels and includes Indonesian movies (some with English subtitles). Tickets are inexpensive and are usually available at the door.

Eating in Jakarta
Indonesia offers an exotic mix of cuisines. The heritage includes regional specialities as well as Dutch, Arabic, Chinese, Malay and more recent Western fads.

Jakarta has a variety of Western-style restaurants, but you will pay dearly to eat at international hotels. Dinner in a local restaurant will cost barely 15 per cent as much.

Good, cheap places to eat are small, seemingly improvised street restaurants where you sit on a bench shaded by an awning emblazoned with the 'house' speciality. *Soto* (spicy soup made of either beef or lamb) is a Jakarta favourite. Jalan Taman Sari and Jalan Kendal are popular with gourmets of Indonesian cooking. Restaurants marked 'Padang' serve spicy, regional dishes: try Jalan Kebon Sirih for a good selection. Recommended restaurants are the **Laguna, Nyun Nyun** and **Sari Kuring.** Near the Hyatt Aryaduta, the latter is a huge busy restaurant serving tasty, budget-priced Javanese food. It is excellent for families; go early.

Three more expensive restaurants with good reputations are: **Handayani Restaurant,** Jalan Abdul Muis 36; **Java Gardens,** Jalan AM Sangaji 15A; **Oasis Restaurant,** Jalan Raden Saleh Raya 47. The last-mentioned is almost a Jakarta institution. Built as a house by a millionaire Dutchman during the Raffles period, it serves mainly Western dishes in elegant, colonial-style surroundings. *Rijstaffel* (Dutch colonial food) is also a 'house speciality'. Dress up.

Seafood

The **Nelayyan Restaurant** in the Hotel Borobodur Inter-Continental offers a daily seafood buffet.

Ideal for families, is the big **Pinisi Floating Restaurant** moored off Ancol Park. Each

A wide variety of foods can be found on the Indonesian menu

*Late-night eating is a speciality at
Jakarta's many warung*

deck specialises in different
seafood – Western, Chinese or
Japanese. Expensive.
The **Nelayyan, Seafood Market
and Restaurant** on Jalan Jendral
Gatot Subroto is cheaper.

Warung
Warung, alfresco restaurants
open from dusk until 23.00 hrs,
are a feature of Jakarta. A
collection of *warung* is a
pujasera. All serve tasty, cheap
Indonesian or Chinese foods.
There are *warung* everywhere,
but especially good places are
behind the National Museum, in
Glodok (Chintaown), around
Blok M (bus terminal), Pasar
Baru, night market and Jalan
Peenongen, a huge open-air
foodstall area after 18.00 hrs.
Watch out for pickpockets.

Chinese
Jakarta has the best Chinese
restaurants in Indonesia. Good
value are: **Eka Ria** (Cantonese),
Jalan Kemarkmuran; **Fajar**
(Cantonese), Golden Truly
Supermarket, Jalan
Suryopranoto; and **Summer
Palace** (Sechuan), 7th floor,
Tedja Buana Building, Jalan
Menteng, Raya. Others are on
Jalan Gajahmada in Chinatown.

Japanese
Most major hotels have a
Japanese restaurant. The **Shima**
(Hyatt Aryaduta) is considered
Jakarta's best. The **Jakarta
Nippon Kan** (Hilton) is also
good. The **Akasaka Mas,** Duta
Merlin Block D, 4-5 Jalan
Gajahmada is good and cheap.
There is a Japanese fast-food
place on Jalan Agus Salim.

Western
Western cooking in tourist
hotels ranges from awful to
excellent. The best Italian
restaurant is the smart
Ambiente, Mezzanine floor,
Hyatt Aryaduta. The **Taman Sari**
in the Jakarta Hilton serves huge
American steaks. An excellent
steak restaurant is next to the
Delicious Bakery in Chinatown.
For rooftop, western-style
dining, try the **Sahid Grill** (Sahid
Jaya Hotel) and **Nirwana** (Hotel
Indonesia). Dress up.
Popular western restaurants
include:
American Hamburger, Jalan
Melawai IV/17 (tel: 774945).
Art & Curio, Jalan Kebon
Binatang III/8 A (tel: 8322879).
Bavaria, Prince Bld, Jalan
Jendral Sudirman (tel: 586673).
Cafe Expresso, Jalan Kemang
Raya 3A (tel: 797754).

Casablanca, Kuningan Plaza, Jalan HR Rasuna Said Kuningan (tel: 514800, 5781175).

Casa Pub, Jalan Sidoardjo 1 (tel: 356559).

Castelo Do Mar, Jalan Kemang Raya 6A, Kebayoran (tel: 791316).

Church Texas Fried Chicken, Jalan Samanhudi No 14-16.

Club Noerdwijk, Jalan Ir H Juanda 5A (tel: 353909).

East-West Barbeque, Lina Building, 6th floor, Jalan H R Rasuna Said Kuningan (tel: 587731 ext 205, 582283).

Front Page, Jalan Merdeka Selatan (Wisma Antara Building) (tel: 348045).

Gandy Steak House, Jalan Gajahmada 82A (tel: 622127, 620539), Jalan Melawai VIII/2 (tel: 774337), Jalan HOS Cokroaminoto (tel: 333292).

Kallista Restaurant & Lounge, Jalan Panglima Polim Raya 35 (tel: 714696, 773056).

Kelapa Gading, Kelapa Gading Sports Centre (tel: 4896804).

Kemang Hill, Jalan Kemang Raya 14 (tel: 792605).

Kentucky Fried Chicken, Jalan Melawai Raya 84 (tel: 731463), Jalan Cikini Raya 119 (tel: 321045), Jalan Gajahmada (tel: 356947), Jalan Agus Salim 31-33 (tel: 322035), Ratu Plaza, Jalan Jendral Sudirman (tel: 712182).

La Bodega, Jalan Terogong Raya – Cilandak (tel: 767798).

La Fonda, Jalan Ir H Juanda 4B (tel: 365390).

Le Bistro, Jalan Wahid Hasyim 75 (tel: 364272).

Melawai Barbeque, Jalan Melawai Raya No 7.

Memories, Wisma Indocement, Ground Floor Jalan Jendral Sudirman (tel: 5781008).

Orleans, Jalan Adityawarman 67 (tel: 715695).

Permata Hijau, Wisma Bakrie, Ground Floor, Jalan HR Rasuna Said (tel: 510132).

Pete's Club, Gunung Sewu Building, Jalan Jendral Gatot Subroto (tel: 515478).

Pinocchio, Wisma Metropolitan I, Top Floor, Jalan Jendral Sudirman (tel: 514736).

Pizza Hut, Jakarta Theatre Building, Jalan MH Thamrin 9 (tel: 352064, 342049); Pondok Indah, Jalan Lapangan Hijau 3 (tel: 764028); Jalan Let. Jendral Haryono, Tebet (tel: 826096).

Pizza Ria, Hilton Hotel, Jalan Jendral Gatot Subroto (tel: 583051).

Ponderosa (Steak House), Wisma Antara, Jalan Merdeka Selatan (tel: 348045, 342398); South Widjojo Centre, Jalan Jendral Sudirman (tel: 583823, 587731 ext 205, 251); Centre Point Building, Jalan Jendral Gatot Subroto (tel: 5780480, 5780202 ext. 1001, 1002); Arthaloka Building, Jalan Jendral Sudirman (tel: 583280).

Prince, Jalan Blora No 9 (tel: 335369, 337060).

Raffles Tavern, Jalan Jendral Sudirman (Ratu Plaza, 3rd Floor) (tel: 711894).

Rice Bowl, Wisma Nusantara Building, Jalan MH Thamrin (tel: 354912).

Rugantino, Jalan Melawai Raya 28 (tel: 714727).

Shakey's Pizza, Jalan Bulungan 8, Kemayoran Baru (tel: 770288).

The Black Angus, Jalan HOS Cokroaminoto 86A (tel: 331551).

The Club Room, Mandarin Hotel, Jalan MH Thamrin (tel: 359141).

The George & Dragon, Jalan Teluk Betung 32 (tel: 325625).

The Palm Beach, Prince Centre
Building, Jalan Jendral Sudirman
(tel: 586683).
Toba Rotisserie, Borobodur
Inter-Continental Hotel
(tel: 5781659).

Shopping

Handicrafts

Jakarta collects all the
handicrafts of Indonesia and
sells them at prices rather
higher than where they are
made. Most are still
bargain-priced. You can buy
woodcarving from Sumatra,
Sulawesi and Irian Jaya; *batik*
and silverware from Bali.
Exceptional buys are fabrics
and rattan, shells, carved fruits,
fans, *wayang* puppets and
leatherware. Do not bargain in
big department stores.
Elsewhere bargaining is
essential. The **Sarinah
Department Stores** (especially
two floors of crafts in Sarinah
Jaya) are highly recommended;
also **Jakarta Handicraft Centre,**
12A Jalan Pekalangen. **Pasar
Seni Arts** at Ancol is good for
families to browse.
Most large hotels have their
own shopping arcades where
you can purchase handicraft
items. These are also good
places for jewellery, especially
the Borobodur Inter-Continental,
the Sari Pacific, and the Hilton
Hotel bazaar. However, hotel
arcades are expensive – if easy
– places to shop.

Antiques

There are lots of fakes, but
occasional wonderful buys,
including Chinese and
European-style carved furniture,
kris (ceremonial daggers) and

Chinese ceramics. If prices are
the criterion, genuine antiques
are found on Jalan Kebon Sirih,
parallel to Jalan Jaksa, 10
minutes' walk from the Hyatt
Aryaduta hotel.
Djody: No 22. Large expensive
shop for browsing. Also Thai
and Burmese artefacts.
Dornis: No 14. Good objects
from Timor and Kalimantan, plus
glassware and pottery.
Ganesha: No 5A. Unusual
primitive artefacts. Sumatra
specialists.
Liberty: No 12A. Balinese
artefacts, old *batik* prints.
Soni-Art: No 6. Chinese
porcelain, etc.
Jalan Surabaya consists of
several blocks of fascinating
small shops selling everything
from Dutch clocks and ships'
compasses to Sumatran
calendars. Shops 134, 138/9 and
162 are recommended.
Bargaining is vital – the true
price is at least 30 per cent less
than asked. Unlike Bali, there is
no high-pressure salesmanship.
Jalan Surabaya is perfectly safe
for a woman on her own.

General Shopping

Jakarta has several large
department stores which
compare with any in London.
You can buy anything in the
multi-storey **Sarinah Department
Stores** at Jalan MH Thamrin II
and Jalan Iskandarsyah II 2,
Kemayoran Baru. More modern,
the latter is highly
recommended. Do not miss the
4th floor devoted to *batiks* or the
basement supermarket. Open
09.00 – 18.00 hrs.
Gajahmada Plaza, Jalan
Gajahmada, is another exclusive

shopping complex for de luxe imports, jewellery, etc, 10-30 minutes by taxi from central Jakarta. Also in Chinatown, the **Duta Merlin Shopping Centre,** Jalan Gajahmada is recommended. Other good shopping centres are: **Ratu Plaza, Ramayana Department Store** (at several locations in the city), and **Blok M** in the smart suburb of Kemayoran Baru. Take a taxi. A cheap, interesting shopping complex is **Pasar Rama.** Curious visitors may be interested in a vast, wholesale cake auction, held daily there at 03.00-05.00 hrs. You have to be keen. Good general buys (later) are clothes, trainers or gym boots, fruit and vegetables. Addresses of these and other shopping areas and centres are listed below.

Sarinah Department Store, Jalan MH Thamrin No 11 (tel: 327425).
Ratu Plaza, Jalan Jendral Sudirman.
Matahari Department Store, Ratu Plaza shopping centre, 3rd Floor Blok M Shopping Area, Jalan Melawai IV; Pasar Senen Shopping Area, 1st Floor, Pasar Baru Shopping Area; Jatinegara Shopping Area.
Sarinah Jaya Shopping Centre, Jalan Iskandarsyah II/2 (tel: 730171).
Duta Merlin Shopping Centre, Jalan Gajahmada.
Gajahmada Plaza, Jalan Gajahmada.
Ramayana Department Store, Pasar Senen Shopping Area, 2nd Floor (tel: 353677); Blok M Shopping Area (tel: 772595); Jalan Melawai IV/27 (tel: 772191); Jalan Agus Salim No 22A (tel: 337713), where you

Jakarta's markets are lively and interesting, and add to the variety and colour of the city

will get practically anything.
Aldiron Plaza, Jalan Melawai, Kemayoran Baru.
Hayam Wuruk Plaza, Jalan Hayam Wuruk.
Pasar Senen, located at Jalan Pasar Senen, provides all kinds of textiles, electric fixtures, ready made dresses, etc.
Pasar Tanah Abang, not far from Sarinah Department Store. This shopping centre provides all kinds of textiles and *batiks.*

Bookshops/Stationery/ Newspapers
All tourist hotels have a

bookshop selling books about Indonesia, magazines, postcards etc. Prices are often 15-20 per cent more than in outside shops. Near the Hyatt Aryaduta is the **Gunung Agung**, Jakarta's oldest and biggest bookshop and stationers. Better hotels deliver local English-language papers to your room. **Gramedia,** Jalan Gajahmada (Chinatown) and Jalan Melawai (Blok M) has the best English-language selection, but do not depend on finding something of interest. Kwitang district is Jakarta's bookshop area.

Clothes Markets
A lively clothes market is held around the Portuguese cannon on Taman Fatahillah, daily except Sunday, 06.00-15.00 hrs. Also **Manga Dua** Market in Chinatown and Pasar Baru which sells everything as well as fabrics, 'Polo' sportswear, Kelvin Klein copies, and the inevitable Lacoste designs. Indonesia makes excellent, bargain-priced gym-boots. Try **Pasar Rama** – at Senen (Monday).

Cassettes and Photographic
Excellent recordings of Western classical, jazz, rock and pop music, plus Indonesian selections are available at half European prices. There are good shops in Blok M (especially in the Aldiron Plaza) and Jalan Agus Salim. The latter street also has many photographic shops selling all types of film. Even professional film can be bought at **Jakarta Foto,** No 35A. English spoken. Good, cheap, fast developing of prints.

Sport
During your stay in Jakarta you need not miss your favourite sports. There are a number of sport centres and golf courses, and bowling is particularly popular here.

Golf Courses
Jakarta Golf Club, Jalan Rawamangun Muka Raya (tel: 4891208 or 4895298).
Padang Golf Jaya Ancol, Jalan Lodan Timur Ancol (tel: 681121).
Halim Golf Course, Lanuma Halim Perdanakusuma (tel: 800729, 800793).
Kemayoran Golf Course, Jalan Asia Afrika Senayan (tel: 582508, 581695).
Pondok Indah Golf and Country Club, Jalan Metro Pondok Indah, Kemayoran Lama (tel: 764906, 762802, 766962).
Jagorawi Golf and Country Club (tel: 581001).
Sawangan Country Club, Jalan Raya Sawangan – Parung (tel: 742193).

Squash
Courts are available at: Borobodur Inter-Continental Hotel. Jakarta Hilton Hotel and Mandarin Oriental Hotel.

Bowling
Jaya Ancol Bowling Centre. Kartika Chandra Bowling Centre. Monas Bowling Centre and Kemayoran Baru Bowling Centre.

Swimming
Available at international standard hotels; Jaya Ancol Dreamland; Senayan Swimming Pool; Kelapa Gading Sport Centre; Grogol Sport Centre; Kuningan Sport Centre; Taman Mini Indonesia Indah.

WHAT TO SEE ON BALI

Bali has many faces, and the visitor may wish to glimpse all of these or perhaps get to know just one or two. There is certainly something for all interests and the gazetteer that follows gives plenty of detail. But first, a brief description of what Bali has to offer may be helpful in the planning of itineraries.

In the south, the capital **Denpasar** is the main business and administrative centre, and the **Kuta-Legian** and **Sanur-Semawang** areas are popular beach resorts. Watersports, shopping and nightlife are the highlights.

The **Nusa Dua Bukit Peninsula** is an emerald earring off south Bali. It includes an international tourist complex, a port and a rugged coastline. Watersports are enjoyed here, especially surfing off **Ulu Watu.**

Central Bali is the cultural heartland of the island, centred on **Ubud-Mas** and local villages. Here the pleasures are arts and crafts, shopping, lush scenery and beautiful rural walks.

The **East Coast** has picturesque beach resorts with good watersports, especially diving. There are also relics of ancient kingdoms and fine views.

The **West Coast** sees few visitors. Plantation farming is carried out in jungle clearings. The surfing beaches are undeveloped.

The **North Coast** is a drier region with black sand beaches and good diving. This, the area of the old Dutch capital, remains uncommercialised.

The **Central Mountain region** is cool, moist and green with quiet lakes, gently smoking volcanoes and important temples. It is an area for trekking.

Nusa Penida and **Nusa Lembongan** islands off southeast Bali enjoy a rustic lifestyle. Quiet coral islands, they have good surfing.

Notes

Sites such as temples or caves are always accessible to visitors. During normal visiting times (roughly 08.00-18.00 hrs), there may be a custodian on duty to whom you will be expected to pay an entrance fee or donation.

The words *bemo* and *losmen*, which occur throughout the gazetteer, may be unfamiliar. For explanations see pages 121 and 93.

West and Far East come together in the architecture of Agung Karangasem in Amlapura

◆◆
AMLAPURA
East Coast

Amlapura lies inland, 10 minutes from the sea. It is a journey of about three and a half hours from Denpasar via Gianyar and Candi Dasa. Amlapura was known as Karangasem until the eruption of Gunung Agung in 1963. The superstitious Balinese changed its name in the hope of averting another eruption. The town is spread out, with a large, clean residential area and small, downhill business centre.

The Kingdom of Karangasem, which seceded from the Gelgel kingdom in the 17th century, became the most powerful kingdom in Bali. **Agung Karangasem** is an early 20th-century palace also known as Puri Kanginan. It was owned by the last rajas of Karangasem before the Dutch takeover.

Accommodation

Amlapura is not a place to stay. Travellers visit it from either Candi Dasa or Tirtagangga.

Food and Drink

Lenny's is a 'tourist-type' restaurant.

Travelling On

The bus-*bemo* station is at the end of the shopping district where the road descends to Ujung. Buses terminate at Amlapura, but there is a red *bemo*-service on to **Singaraja.** **Tirtagangga** is 15 minutes' drive. The Amlapura-Rendang road is half a mile (1km) out of Amlapura. This is a quiet, less travelled route across to Besakih (the Mother Temple – see page 42) via the market town of **Bebandem.** The short diversion to **Putung** is worth making for the good views on a clear day.

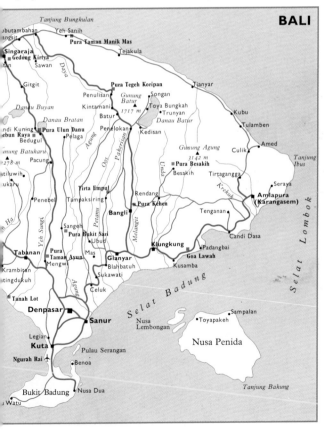

WHAT TO SEE ON BALI

BALINA BEACH See CANDI
DASA

BANGLI
*central-eastern Bali, 26 miles
(42km) from Denpasar*
The town is *en route* to Lake
Batur, halfway up the slope to
Penelokan (see page 63).
Expect traffic congestion until
you pass Gianyar. There is a
good road surface to Penelokan,
and rich farmland scenery.
Today an unprepossessing
town, in the 12th century Bangli
was capital of a Balinese
kingdom. It is worth visiting for
Pura Kehen, a terraced temple,
reached up a long flight of
steps. The temple's walls are
inlaid with the remains of bright
pieces of chipped Chinese
porcelain similar to temple
decoration in Bangkok. The
upper sanctuary has 11 tapering
merus, resting places of the
gods. A shrine houses thrones
for the Hindu deities, Brahma,
Shiva and Vishnu. There is a
small museum.

Accommodation
Bangli is not an overnight stop
but if you need a bed, try the
Artha Sastra in the town centre,
opposite the busy *bemo* station.
A former royal residence, it is a
pleasant traditional-style inn and
is cheap.

Food and Drink
Try the **night market** (opposite
the Artha Sastra).

Entertainment
There are occasional dance
performances and exhibits for
groups in the arts complex,
down the road from Pura
Kehen.

Side-Trips
Bukit Demulih. The hill of this
name is one hour's walk along
the road to Tampaksiring. There
are great rice terraces and
coastal panoramas to view from
the top.
Pura Dalem. This temple of the
dead with grotesque reliefs is
15 minutes' walk on the road to
Gianyar.

Travelling On
There are frequent minibus and
bemo services to surrounding
places of interest, such as
Kintamani 20 miles (33km),
Klungkung 11½ miles (19km),
Besakih 13 miles (21km).
Warning: There have been
incidents involving robbery and
trickery in the Bangli district.
Car-drivers and *bemo*
passengers need to be alert.

BATUBULAN
*central Bali, 6 miles (10km) from
Denpasar*
Here you will see stonemasons
working in roadside factories.
Many antique/second-hand
shops line the busy Ubud-
Gianyar road. **Oka, Antik
Kembar** and **Indra Antiques** are
suggestions, if you are
interested in this kind of
purchase.

BEDUGAL
Central Highlands
The village lies at 5,000 feet
(1,500m) above sea-level, in
Tabanan District and is about
four hours' drive from Denpasar.
Bedugal is on Lake Bratan
which fills the crater of Gunung
Bratan. Cool and peaceful, it is a
perfect foil to the humid coast.

The mountain air of Bedugal village, on Lake Bratan, is refreshingly welcome

Uludanu Temple at Candi Kuning on Lake Bratan just over a mile (2km) north of Bedugal is half-Hindu, half-Buddhist. It is dedicated to Dewi Danu (Goddess of Water).
Bukit Mungsu is an orchid market below Bedugal. Livestock and fruit and vegetables are also sold there.
Kebun Raya, near the market, is a botanical garden and orchid collection.

Accommodation and Eating
Bukit Mungsu Indan. A new hotel, set back from the lake on a hill, it is plain but comfortable. Rear cottages have a wonderful panorama overlooking Bedugal valley. Restaurant and bar. Moderate.
Hotel Bedugal. Picturesque lakeshore location, but spoilt by groups and noisy microphones. Moderately cheap. A restaurant overlooking the lake is pleasant at night. Eat here rather than the restaurant on the hill whose waiter has to trudge down (and up) with every order.
Lila Graha (tel: 25750). This lofty spot above the lake is potentially charming. It has a restaurant and bar. Moderately cheap.
Pancasari Inn (tel: 34875/33962). Thirty minutes' walk from the lake, it has 11 de luxe rooms. Peaceful and comfortable with restaurant and bar; tennis, golf course near by. Suitable for couples rather than solitary travellers. Expensive.

Activities
You can walk around lakes Bratan, Tablingan and Buyan, about 16½ miles (27km). Swimming in the lakes is a chilly experience. If fishing is your scene, rod and worms can be bought locally. Boating trips by speedboat (minimum four persons) or motorised *prahu*

can be made at a cost.
Bali Handara Kosaido Country
Club has an 18-hole golf course
in a glorious setting.

Travelling On
There are *bemo* connections to
Singaraja, Denpasar, etc.

◆
BENOA
Nusa Dua Bukit peninsula
Bali's small port lies on the tip of
a shallow bay at the end of the
airport runway, 20 minutes'
drive south of Sanur. The Bali
International Yacht Club will
interest anyone wanting to
crew: it boasts a notice board,
clean WCs and a small licensed
restaurant. There are *prahus* for
rent to visit Serangan Island –
expensive.

◆◆
BESAKIH
central-northeastern Bali,
37 miles (60km) from Denpasar
The first mention of **Pura
Besakih** is AD1007. It has been
the central Balinese 'Mother
Temple' since the 15th-century
Gelgel dynasty. The temple
complex is 3,300 feet (1,000m)
up Gunung Agung. Steep twin
stairways ascend seven rising
terraces containing about 30
different shrines. Visitors are
forbidden to enter the inner
courtyards. Besakih is
disappointing, even melancholic
on a dull, misty day.

Getting There
There is a frequent *bemo*
service from Klungkung, and
Besakih is also approached from
Bangli, or Tirtagangga.
Self-drivers take the left fork
(ignore the 'No Entry' sign), half
a mile (1km) before the top. You

will be charged for parking and
on entry a donation will be
requested.
It is a steep walk from the
ticket-house up to the temple.
Easy-riders charge a fee to
pillion you to the base on
motorcycles. Ride up and walk
down. You have to run the
gauntlet of souvenir sellers,
whose shops line the path to the
temple. The trip is tough for
older travellers.

Accommodation
Three miles (5km) below
Besakih is the simple **Arca
Valley Inn,** which is a base for
the climb up Gunung Agung
(see below).

Food and Drink
The parking lot is ringed by
clean cafés. Stalls sell bananas,
salak and *mangosteen* (see
page 89).

Climbing Gunung Agung
The volcano is over 10,000 feet
(3,000m) high, and rises six
miles (10km) behind Besakih.
Fit climbers should manage the
trip in 10 hours. Basic
requirements are: a flashlight,
weatherproof jacket, good
walking boots, water and
supplies such as sweets or fruits.
Depart at 05.00 hours to get
back before dusk and take a
guide as lower trails are
confusing in the dark. Much of
the ascent is vertical; the middle
section traverses humid jungle
and the upper part is over
lichen-covered rocks. The final
ridge is narrow and there is
room only for one person at a
time to stand on the summit. But
there is never a crowd. The
peak is very cold and you

should take into account that rain may obscure the view. The volcano remains active – the last eruption was 16 May 1963. Alternatively, make it a two-day trip and stay overnight on the mountainside, at **Tirtha Mas,** where holy water is collected (ask your guide).

◆
BLAHBATUH
East Coast
Inland junction for Gianyar, Bona. The **Pura Gaduh** temple here is a reconstruction – the original was destroyed in an earthquake in 1917. It houses an ancient stone head, reputedly portraying Kebo Iwa, a legendary giant.

◆
BONA
central Bali
About 12½ miles (20km) from Denpasar, on a back road between Gianyar and Blahbatuh, the village itself is insignificant, but bamboo furniture is an important industry. Woven palm-leaf articles are another local product. You can see a *kechak* (see page 96) and other dances there – tickets and transport from Ubud.

◆
BUKIT JAMBA
central Bali
This is a scenic point, five miles (8km) north of Klungkung *en route* to Besakih on a quiet road. It has a garden restaurant and WC on the right, up steep steps. Stop at the lay-by opposite the restaurant for a view down the valley, to the sea.

Fishing and sailing are popular activities in Candi Dasa

◆◆
CANDI DASA
East Coast
The journey takes about 1½-2 hours from Denpasar. Traffic is bad until Klungkung. There is coastal scenery from Kusamba. A quiet fishing village until recently, Candi Dasa now counts more than 50 *losmens*, restaurants and ancillaries to a tourist trade. It is not yet spoilt like Kuta, but this seems likely. The village of Candi Dasa stretches for a mile (2km) along the palm-fringed coast. A drawback is no beach. At high tide the sand disappears and you must sunbathe on rough sea walls. A small lagoon by the Amlapura exit marks the end of

town. There is a bank, post office and several souvenir shops.

Accommodation

Candi Dasa is a good alternative sightseeing base to Kuta, or Sanur, although it is more for younger travellers. Check that your room, the restaurant, or bar is not falling into the sea. Erosion is bad along the seafront.

Candi Dasa Beach Bungalows. Pleasant, but as with many hotels, the bungalows are too close together. Moderate to cheap.

Homestay Ida. Pleasant, airy cottages by the lagoon. Moderate.

Rama Lakeside Bungalows. On a picturesque lagoon site. The upstairs rooms are more private; ask for Room 1. Moderate to cheap.

Rama Ocean View Bungalows. Modern cottage complex catering to tour-groups. Moderate.

An option is to stay outside Candi Dasa at **Balina Beach,** two miles (3km) away, where there is excellent swimming, sailing and diving.

Nelayan Village Bungalows/Balina Diving Centre, Office: Jalan Raya Batujimbar 129, Sanur, Bali (telex: 35307). A variety of rooms from cheap to family-style suites. Pleasant and comfortable, with a restaurant and bar. The centre specialises in diving and guests are mainly divers. There are qualified Scuba instructors, and an

The Puri Buitan Hotel at Balina Beach is run with families in mind

advanced open-water dive
course of four to five days is
available. English, German,
Dutch spoken. Advance
booking required.
Puri Buitan Hotel, PO Box 444,
Denpasar (tel: (361) 87182).
New, clean, modern hotel on
the beach with 34 simple
fan-cooled rooms. Excellent
management. Ideal for families.
Tours arranged. Licensed
restaurant. Swimming pool.

Food and Drink
Candi Dasa lacks good
restaurants. Eating is very much
a hit and miss affair.
Ibu Rasmini Warung near the
lagoon has a cheap, Indonesian-
style menu with *nasi goreng* etc.
Seafood is hard to find. **TJ's** is a
more expensive restaurant in
central Candi Dasa. Tables are
on platforms set around
fish-ponds. Eclectic menu and
loud music.
The **Hawaii Restaurant** is
disappointing.

Nightlife
There are several bars and two
low-key discos. People
generally go to bed early in
Candi Dasa.

Activities
Scuba Diving is available off
offshore islets; see also Balina
Diving Centre above (under
Accommodation).
Snorkelling fans can observe
reef life in safe conditions about
100 yards/metres off shore.
There is excellent **swimming**
from Balina Beach, and for
sailing enthusiasts *prahus* are
available at Balina Beach, or
from Candi Dasa lagoon.
You can **walk** to Balina Beach

(2 miles/3km) or, alternatively,
inland to Tenganan (4 miles/6km
– see page 69).
Short road trips can be made to
Amlapura, Tirtagangga and
Besakih.

Shopping
The souvenir shops are
harbingers of Kuta-style
commerce (see page 57). There
is *ikat*-weaving in Tenganan
(see page 69).

◆◆
CANGGU
*Southwest Coast about 7½ miles
(12km) from Denpasar*
A lovely road-trip through the
rice-fields ends on a black sand
surfing beach – the reason for
visiting Canggu. Stay on the
main road: side-roads are
terrible. A name without any
apparent village, Canggu has
one basic hotel:
Perenan Beach Hotel. Four
rooms with shared bathroom/
WC. Simple restaurant with
drinks. No telephone. Often full.
Ideal for backpackers or surfies.
Not for anyone else.

◆◆
CELUK
*Central southeastern Bali about
40 minutes from Denpasar.*
Celuk is Bali's silver centre.
Take your pick of dozens of
workshops along the road. A
quiet place to watch
silversmiths is Cemengan
Village. Most designs are
traditional, but some are
influenced by Western tastes.
Coming from Denpasar, turn left
at a roadsign 'Ana' and continue
110 yards (100m). See the
silversmiths, walk around the
village and visit the temple.

◆ CULIK

Northeast Coast

This is a transit stop on the
Tirtagangga-Tulamben road.
There are rice-terraces and
views of Gunung Agung (see
page 42). Beyond Culik, the old
lava flow from the volcano
descends right down to the sea.
For anyone feeling the need for
a quick dip, there is a beach
near Culik village.

◆◆ DENPASAR

southern Bali

The capital and main town,
(population around 300,000),
Denpasar used to be a
charming old tree-lined town,
where people commuted by
dokar, or donkey-cart. The
name *den pasar* means 'beside
the market'. Dusty, noisy and
polluted by traffic fumes, it is
now a place travellers avoid.

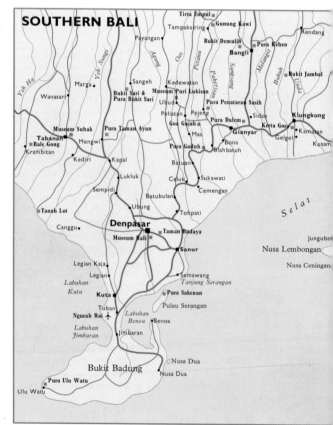

Allow Denpasar one day: it has some fine museums.

Sightseeing

Bali Museum
Jalan May Wisnu, off Puputan Square
Founded by the Dutch in 1932, separate pavilions feature traditional temple and palace architecture. In the second courtyard, is a large building in the style of an old royal pavilion

of the Karangasem kingdom. Styles from Singaraja and Tabanan are also represented. Exhibits range from Balinese stone-age artefacts to modern works. Special features are stone sculptures, dance masks and scale models of ceremonial events. Towering Barong Landung figures are represented (see page 96). *Open:* Tuesday, Wednesday, Thursday, Sunday 08.00–14.00hrs; and Friday 08.00–11.00 hrs; Saturday 08.00–12.30hrs. Closed Monday.

Taman Budaya (Art Centre)
Easily found on Jalan Nusa Indah in east Denpasar, its galleries include a permanent exhibition of Balinese painting. The centre is set in picturesque grounds and the complex includes open-stage dance performances *Open:* Tuesday to Sunday, 08.00–17.00hrs. Entry charge. A Festival of Arts each June-July features *gamelan*, dances and traditional Balinese skills.

Central Market
This is across the stream from the original *Pasar Badung*. It is dark and hot, but filled with fascinating stalls. Go before 08.00 hours. Try typical snacks.

Temples
While Denpasar is a busy commercial centre, temple worship continues unperturbed. Many temples are hidden. Others, like **Pura Melanting**, the market temple, are obvious. Market vendors pause here to make offerings before work. Adjacent to the Bali Museum, **Pura Jagatnata** is dedicated to

WHAT TO SEE ON BALI

Enticing displays of fruit and veg in Denpasar's Central Market

the supreme god, Ida Batara Sanghyang Widi Wasa. His coral throne is mounted on a cosmic turtle and *naga* serpents. The best plan is not to devote too much time to temples in Denpasar as they are two a penny in the countryside.

Accommodation
You are unlikely to want to stay in Denpasar, but one hotel eases you nicely into Bali from overseas:
Bali Hotel, Jalan Veteran 3, Denpasar 8011 (tel: (0361) 25681). Denpasar's original old downtown hotel, built in 1927, has a lingering colonial atmosphere. There are 74 large, plain rooms, a swimming pool and gardens. Moderate.
Others are:
Adi Yasa, Jalan Nakula II. Within walking distance of the centre

of town, it is pleasant, but no longer the traveller's refuge of yesteryear. Cheap.
Hotel Denpasar, Jalan Diponegoro 103, Denpasar 80113 (tel: 28336). Cottage-style rooms. Guests mainly Indonesian. Moderate.

Food and Drink
At dusk *warung* (foodstalls) mushroom everywhere. **Pasar Senggol** ('Night Market', open 16.00-20.00 hours) is a good eating spot. Other centres are around bus and *bemo* stations and near the Wisata Theatre in Jalan Diponegoro. The latter sells delicious Muslim-made *satés* in rich, thick peanut sauce. Good Chinese food is to be had at **Restoran Puri Selua,** Jalan Gajahmada 16: more expensive, but air-conditioned. **Goyalli** is a cheap, fast-food restaurant with bar near the Indra Cinema. The **Bali Hotel** has an extensive Indonesian-European menu.

Nightlife
There is no Kuta-type entertainment. Evening dances *(kechak)* are performed at 18.30 hours nightly at the Art Centre. Go early to avoid coachloads. There is a female singer at the **Bali Hotel.**

Shopping
Denpasar sells crafts from all over Bali, but they are more expensive than in their places of origin. Crafts shops on Jalan Gajahmada sell paintings, carvings, etc. Above the Central Market, **Kumbasari Shopping Centre** sells handicrafts plus a lot of junk.
The government co-operative

centre **Sanagraha Kriya Asta**
(tel: (0361) 22942) is in Tohpati,
on the road to Batubulan. It is
recommended for good quality
woodcarving, painting, *batik*
and silverware at fixed prices.
Free transport is provided from
and to your hotel in the
Denpasar – Sanur – Kuta area.
Open: Monday to Saturday
09.00-17.30hrs.
Mega is a good shop next door
with a branch at Jalan
Gajahmada 36 in Denpasar.

Getting About
There are *bemo* services
between the bus stations (see
below) and Jalan Gajahmada,
the main street. Self-drive is not
recommended without a guide
and remains a hair-raising
experience. *Dokars*, pony-traps,
are fun if you can find one. Dust,
traffic and open drains make
walking stressful.

Travelling On

Bus Stations
Denpasar has four main
bus/*bemo* stations for travel
to all parts of Bali:
Tegal (Kuta road) southern
peninsula.
Ubung (Gilimanuk road) north
and west. Main station for Java.
Kereneng (Tohpati road) east
and central Bali.
Suci (central Denpasar) mainly
to Benoa. Location of many
Surabaya (Java) bus-lines and
agents.
Other *bemo* terminals are (not
much used by tourists):
Sanglah (south Denpasar) for
Benoa Port.
Wangaya (north Denpasar) for
travel north, to the Sangeh
Monkey Forest.

If you are staying in
Kuta-Legian, buy your bus-ticket
for a journey on from Denpasar
from a local travel agent. The
small extra charge saves hassle
on the day.
Cost of your journey depends
on the type of bus – *bemo*,
micro-bus, or full-size vehicle.
No fare on Bali should exceed
Rp2,000. If buying from the bus
company go early to obtain a
window-seat. Many agents are
located on Jalan Hasanudin in
Denpasar.
Transfers between bus-stations
are by *bemo*.

◆
GIANYAR
southeastern Bali
A 20-minute drive from
Denpasar, Gianyar District is
famous for cottage industries,
especially textiles (visitors may
watch a sarong being woven),
but the town itself is without
interest.
About two miles (3km) north of
the town is the **Pura Dalem**
(temple of the dead), a good
example of temple carving.

◆
GILIMANUK
northwestern tip of Bali
This quiet old town is strung
along Jalan Raya, the road to the
ferry-crossing for Java. Few
travellers stop and there are no
tourist facilities . . . not even
cold beer.
For anyone interested in natural
history, the local mangrove
swamps are rich in wildlife (see
Peace and Quiet page 86), and
the national park of Pulau
Menjangan is off the coast near
Gilimanuk. There is good diving
off the island.

WHAT TO SEE ON BALI

Accommodation/Food and Drink
'Jalak Putih' (the manager is unsure of the name) is about six miles (10km) east on the Lovina Road. Eight simple, but spotless bungalows, with an exterior WC and shower (you pull a cork in a bucket) in an attractive site in a coconut plantation. The beach is black sand, but white beaches are accessible by *prahu*. There is good fishing, diving and windsurfing. Not well placed for general sightseeing, but one of the nicest spots on Bali. Italian-Indonesian menu. Licensed.

Ferry–Java. Buses connect with the steamer and car-ferry. The crossing takes 20 minutes and there are no formalities other than a ticket.

◆
GITGIT
northern Bali
The waterfall near the Singaraja – Bedugal road is a short detour from Gitgit village through lush paddy-fields. You can swim in the pool at the foot of the falls.

◆
GOA GAJAH
central Bali
The 'Elephant Cave' is a former Buddhist retreat, created in the 11th century. There are interior carvings, and a boy with a light will point out niches where the monks probably meditated. Admission charge. Hasslers are a nuisance.

◆
GOA LAWAH
East Coast, about 2 miles (3km) east of Klungkung
This is the 'Bat Cave', with thousands of bats and said to extend all the way to Besakih, 18 miles (30km) away. If you stop, accept no 'gifts' of necklaces, etc, and take no pictures, unless you are prepared to pay. There are charges for parking and entry.

GUNUNG AGUNG see BESAKIH

◆◆◆
GUNUNG BATUR/ LAKE BATUR
Central Mountains
This active volcano and crater lake lie at 5,630 feet (1,717m) in Bangli District, about four hours' drive from Denpasar. A branch road from Besakih is drivable, but badly pot-holed.
Lake Batur is a large, deep, green lake lying on the eastern side of the volcano in the outer crater rim. In the old days you had to walk or ride down by

horse from Penelokan (see page 63). The road is now tar, the macadam laid across the lava flow, making the 35-minute journey a thrilling roller-coaster ride. Sound your horn on the blind crests. There is a *bemo* service from Penelokan to the hot springs at Toya Bungkah. If you want to take to the water, Kedisan is the lake boat-terminal, with charter-boats (seating 12). Do not hire a dug-out and paddle yourself: Lake Batur is larger than it looks and storms are common. The best time for sightseeing is before 10.00 hours. Take a warm weatherproof coat.

Toya Bungkah (Tirtha) is the main tourist village on Lake Batur, a bleak settlement with

Batur volcano looms over the deep waters of Lake Batur

about a dozen *losmen*, built from volcanic rock. Local hot springs are a reviver if you have walked up Gunung Batur (see below). Locals are unfriendly and solitary women may not feel comfortable. Young people often make Toya Bungkah a base for climbing the volcano. See also **Kintamani** page 52.

Climbing Gunung Batur

Climbing Batur volcano is a different proposition to tackling Gunung Agung. The ascent is steep, but fit people should accomplish it without stress. It takes two to three hours to make the ascent to the 2,300-foot (700m) summit, and one and a half hours to descend. The most popular ascent is from Toya Bungkah; a guide is unnecessary. Choose one of the numerous well-indicated tracks and walk straight up. Take a sweater, although it is generally hot. Start by 06.00 hours, to be back for a late lunch. There are drinks stands on the way up if you are flagging. You can walk all around the crater rim to the point of descent at Purajati. Wisps of smoke indicate activity deep within the volcano – Batur last erupted in 1963. There are magnificent views on a clear day.

Accommodation

Balai Seni Toya Bungkah Art Centre. In a quiet spot, this is the only really pleasant place to stay – in detached bungalows with verandahs. It has a restaurant and library. Moderate.

Homestay Nyoman Mawa – 'Under the Volcano'. Near the hot springs. A good base from which to climb Gunung Batur. Cheap.

Losmen Tirta Yatra. Above the hot springs, it attracts backpackers. Cheap.

Segara Homestay. With 29 modest rooms, above the lake, it is five minutes' walk from the boat-terminal. Has a restaurant. Cheap.

Food and Drink

'Under the Volcano' and **Nyoman Pangus Warung** provide local barbecued fish. No fancy meals. Beer available.

◆
GUNUNG KAWI

central Bali, 1 mile (1.5km) from Tampaksiring

These royal temples, or memorials, probably date from the 11th century. They are carved into cliffs with a river flowing between, and form one of Bali's most impressive sites. Legend says the carvings were completed in one night by a giant using his fingernails. The memorials – 10 in all – are among the earliest examples of Balinese art – Goa Gajah (see page 50) is another early site. You must climb hundreds of stairs to reach the complex.

◆
JATILUWIH

central Bali

The name means 'truly marvellous', and the views of rice-terraces justify it. The village is on the slopes of Gunung Batukau, one of Bali's highest peaks. As with most view-points in Bali, you have to gamble on clear weather when you are actually in the vicinity. Jatiluwih is off the tourist track.

◆◆◆
KINTAMANI

Central Mountains

About four hours direct from Denpasar, or two hours south of Singaraja, Kintamani, Penelokan and Batur almost merge into a line of drab, wind-blown shops spread around the crater rim of Gunung Batur.

Kintamani is an important market town and fruit-growing area. Stay overnight to see sunrise and clearing mists over Lake Batur. There is a colourful market every three days, and an occasional performance of the strange *Sanghyang* trance dance (see page 98).

Accommodation

If you decide to stay, Kintamani has mercifully fewer touts than Penelokan (see page 63), but you may be disturbed by dogs... or by cocks calling to each other in the caldera. Most *losmen* are too drab to recommend.

Pay more for warmth and comfort at the **Hotel Puri Astini** which has private bathrooms, and excellent views and is moderately expensive. It is a detour of about half a mile (1km) off the main road to the north of Kintamani (signposted).

Also in the northern end of town is the small, but friendly – for this area – **Hotel Miranda.** You will need warm clothes.

Food and Drink

You can eat in the hotels. **Miranda** has reasonable food and an open fire.

Shopping

Basketware and sarongs are genuine. Trash is in plentiful supply.

*Good battles against Evil in the
Kerta Gosa in Klungkung*

Activities

Using Kintamani as a base, you
can hike up Gunung Batur (see
also page 51), or walk down to
Lake Batur. A guide is
unnecessary – but alone you will
be pestered. Get up early to
make a boat-trip to Trunyan
village (see page 71).

Travelling On

A *bemo* shuttle service runs
between Kintamani and
Penelokan. Onward bus
connections to Ubud/Gianyar-
Denpasar and Singaraja.

◆◆◆
KLUNGKUNG

*East Coast, 25 miles (40km) from
Denpasar*
Traffic is very bad until this
point. Klungkung is a major road
junction for Besakih and the
northeast coast to Amlapura.
While noisy and busy,

Klungkung is of considerable
historic interest. Allow 40
minutes for leisurely
sightseeing, or one and half
hours if you include Kamasan.
Klungkung was where
descendants of the Majapahit
Dynasty established a new
kingdom after fleeing from Java.
They first ruled from Gelgel,
two miles (3km south), and in
1710 moved to Klungkung. The
old Gelgel dynasty ruled Bali for
600 years, when Klungkung was
a flourishing arts centre. Like
the rajas of Badung, the royal
families of Klungkung
committed suicide rather than
capitulate to the Dutch. Most of
Bali's nobility trace lineage to
the 'Dewa Agung', the 'Great
Lord' of Klungkung.
One of the main sights of the
town is the **Kerta Gosa**.
Surrounded by a moat, this Hall
of Justice, stands on the right
corner of the main intersection
of streets in the town centre.

WHAT TO SEE ON BALI

The Balinese equivalent of the Supreme Court, it settled disputes not agreed at village level. Defendants were judged by three priests. Terrifying panels depicting the horrors of hell cover the walls and ceilings. The murals are painted in 'wayang' style, with figures in profile, the symbolism of right and left equating Good and Evil. Adjoining the Kerta Gosa is the Bale Kambang or 'Floating Pavilion'. Both buildings are a reminder of the refined lifestyle of the ancient kingdom of Klungkung.
Open: daily. Parking and admission charges.

Accommodation
You are unlikely to want to stay in Klungkung. Among several poor *losmen* is the **Ramayana Palace,** on the road to Amlapura. Nine very simple rooms. It is better to stay in Ubud or Candi Dasa (see pages 74 and 44).

Food and Drink
Eat at the **Ramayana Palace**, or the 'night market'.

Shopping
Several crafts shops are found on Jalan Diponegoro: try No 241. Hawkers in the parking-lot sell copies of paintings in the Kerta Gosa. If you fancy the style, you would do better to buy one in Kamasan (see below), where local artists perpetuate old-style Gelgel painting.

Side-Trips
Kamasan Village, 2½ miles (4km) south, beyond Gelgel. Here you can buy traditional paintings – basically linear, in browns, ochres and greens. Purists searching for a painting in Bali should consider these.
Kusamba, 15 minutes north. This is a small fishing village on a black sand beach. Roadside scenery shows evidence of the 1963 eruption of Gunung Agung, when lava buried villages and fields. North of Kusamba, a road leads to a salt-panning village.

◆
KRAMBITAN
West Coast, 3.5 miles (6km) inland from Klatingdukuh
A detour of about six miles (10km) from Tabanan, Krambitan has ancient royal palaces and traditionally designed buildings, set off by beautiful flowering shrubs. Off the tourist track, but there is a regular *bemo* service from Tabanan.

◆◆
KUTA (see also Legian)
Southwest Coast, 10 minutes from Denpasar Airport
This is Bali's biggest beach resort, with a strong Australian bias. There are bars, cafés and discos by the dozen; hotels by the hundreds. Kuta is for young ragers into surfing, drinking and generally having a good time. Backpackers like it, as competition keeps prices down. Other people regret they bought a Kuta holiday. Kuta's broad, white beach stretches some six miles (10km) from Tuban past Legian in the north. Behind the main beach is a large area of shops, art markets, pubs, discos, travel agents and rent-a-car-bike-jeep, or -tour. Without traffic Kuta might be fun, but walking is

made an ordeal by motorcycles and hustlers importuning you to buy. Jalan Legian – the route to Denpasar – is perpetually blocked by traffic. The best way to commute is via the lanes, or *gangs*, although not late at night. Drunken Australians have given Kuta a reputation for easy pickings. Most incidents do not involve Balinese.

Activities
Kuta has a splendid surf. The best period is March – July. Australian-trained Balinese lifesavers patrol the beach between the flags – there are dangerous rips at the Legian end. Joggers should get out early before motorcyclists begin riding up and down the sand. There is an entry charge for the main beach. You can buy anything you want without moving: drinks, fruits, snacks, T-shirts, suntan oil, umbrellas. You can even have a massage; and women will also plait your hair. Bargain as if your life depends on it.

Accommodation
To enjoy Kuta, find a quiet hotel near the beach and your evening meal. Cheap *losmens* are popular and advance bookings are difficult.
Arena's Cottages, off Poppies Lane. Small bungalows within walking distance of the beach. Cheap.
Ayu Beach Inn, Poppies Lane (tel: (0361) 51664). Clean, airy rooms. Cheap.
Mandara Cottages, (tel: (0361) 51775). The cottages are behind the beach, in Kuta south-side. Five minutes from the airport and 700 metres from shops.

A swarm of hawkers settles around a likely customer on Kuta Beach

Garden. Asian-European food. Expensive.
Poppies, (tel: (0361) 51059). In Poppies Lane, off Jalan Legian, this is a little gem in central Kuta, out of earshot of the din. Twenty thatched cottages with fans, or air conditioning. Clean, in beautiful gardens around a pool. You can walk to the beach. Expensive. Poppies has some cheaper cottages (without a pool) near by.
Yasa Samudra, main beach (tel: (0361) 51562). Forty rooms, around a small pool. Good for families. More expensive rooms have air conditioning. Licensed restaurant/bar.

Food and Drink
Like you should with accommodation, walk around and check restaurant menus. Small, back-lane *warung* (foodstalls) are most authentic.

WHAT TO SEE ON BALI

Street-side restaurants offer 'international cuisine' with 'Down Under' specialities – roast dinners, jaffles, Vegemite! Shop around for bargain breakfasts: watered-down fruit juice, bacon and eggs, tea and toast. **Made's Warung** on Jalan Pantai Kuta (near Bemo Corner) has meals and snacks throughout the day and night. Walking to the beach from 'Bemo Corner', it is on the right: a good spot to people-watch. There are freshly baked croissants, etc at **Zas** on Jalan Legian, near the Hotel Legian Gardens.

Poppies Cottages offer peace and quiet in central Kuta

Where to eat dinner is more difficult to recommend. **Poppies** stylish garden restaurant has an international menu and is licensed. **Mini's Restaurant,** also on Jalan Legian serves seafood, but go early for a table. **Lenny's** on Jalan Pantai Kuta is another seafood restaurant, moderate, but inconsistent. **Dayu II,** opposite the Bar Casablanca, does reasonable steak and grilled fish.

Other tourist-type restaurants are found on Jalan Bakung Sari. **Gantina Baru** in this area specialises in *padang* food from West Sumatra. **Depot Viva** on Jalan Legian, open-roof, serves Indonesian food.

Kuta has a Kentucky Fried Chicken, several pizza restaurants and ice-cream parlours.

Nightlife

It is unfair not to say that many young tourists find Kuta's nightlife terrific. Others find it banal.

Pub-Crawls are popular entertainment. Buses take increasingly drunken revellers on a local pub-tour. Tickets are sold by attractive Aussie sheilas in Kuta-Legian cafés. You can pay for pick-up and return to your hotel. Popular pubs are **Koala Blue, Bali Billabong,** and **Norm's Bar.** As the night wears on, drinking competitions and ladies wet T-shirt contests become more vulgar.

Some places have a 'happy hour' (18.00-22.00 hrs) when drinks are often 30 per cent less. Try the **Bali Balance Bar.** Or enjoy Kuta's famous sunset over cocktails in a beachfront hotel. Even the pricey **Bali Oberoi** at Legian Beach discounts cocktails by 20 per cent between 18.30 and 19.30 hours.

Discos: what is flavour of the month at time of writing may have fallen from favour now. Favourite discos of the moment are **Peanuts** and **Spotlight** on Jalan Legian; **Gado-Gado** near the beach at the Seminyak end; **Barong**; and **Double Six.** All feature loud Western pop music from 22.00 hours. Entrance fee includes a weak alcoholic beverage of your choice.

Shopping

Kuta is the fashion capital of Indonesia. Every second shop sells flashy 'beach-style' clothing. Eclectic Balinese-Bondi designed T-shirts and board-shorts are bargain buys. Avoid stuff sold by hustlers as designs are not colourfast. So-called 'art markets' – lots of cheaper shops crowded together in a lane – flog down-market goods. Australians trying on leather jackets over their swimming costumes are one of Kuta's peculiar sights. Cassettes are good buys: **Top 10,** (Jalan Melasti 118, in Legian) is recommended. With clothes shops and money-changers, *quik-foto* print shops are prolific. Films are processed cheaply and quite reliably – **Bali Foto Centre,** on Jalan Pantai Kuta, is your best bet. Balinese arts and crafts are sold everywhere. Javanese hustling silver jewellery and fake watches are a nuisance. **Krishna**

Books is a newsagent bookshop in Jalan Legian, with a good selection of travel books. Postcards and stamps are obtainable from a kiosk in Jalan Legian. Check exchange rates at several different money-changers.

Post Office: the main post office, 'Kantor Pas', is near the 'night market', off Jalan Raya Kuta.

Transport

Bemos. Start from 'Bemo Corner', to Denpasar. To Sanur, you must go via Denpasar and change from Tegal to Kereneng. Find companions to charter direct to Sanur. There is a service from the airport to Kuta.

Motorcycles. Local youths earn their living taking pillion passengers between Kuta and Legian. You should wear a safety helmet.

Renting. Many *losmen* have motorcycles, or push-bikes, for rent. They are also parked outside travel agents. Bicycles are best for local sightseeing.

Taxis are the usual means of transport for visitors between airport and hotel (10-15 minutes' drive). Extra charge for luggage – negotiable.

◆
LEGIAN

Like Kuta, Legian was discovered by the 'flower people' of the 1960s. The two villages now merge – the *bemo* connection along Jalan Legian takes five minutes. The main street, Jalan Melasti, has Kuta-style travel agents, art markets and boutiques. There are plenty of hustlers too. North Legian, towards Seminyak, remains undeveloped jungle fringing the beach.

Accommodation

Check out *losmen* in the lanes on the north side of Jalan Melasti. **Sri Beach Inn** in an orchid garden and **Janji Inn** in a coconut grove are possibilities, but there are several others that might fit your particular bill.

If luxury is what you are after, try: **Bali Oberoi**, Jalan Kayu Aya (PO Box 351, Denpasar 8000). Tel: (0361) 51061. Sophistication, quality and style summarise the 75-room Oberoi owned by the Indian hotel group. It has large air-conditioned bungalows with superb beds and sunken marble baths; de luxe Presidential villas have a private swimming pool. First class food. Complimentary daily shuttle service for shopping in Kuta. Quiet, beachfront location in Seminyak – stray dogs are shot. Three cheers for the Bali Oberoi! Very expensive.

Nightlife

Most nightlife centres around Jalan Melasti. **Double Six** and **Gado Gado** are popular discos.

◆◆
LOVINA
North Coast, 6 miles (10km) west of Singaraja

Derived from 'love' and 'ina', which means pleasure, Lovina is the over-all name for a string of black sand beaches – Anturan, Kalibukbuk, Lovina, and others. It has a laid-back lifestyle with cheap, friendly hotels and activities, such as watersports, walking and cycling, making it ideal for families. However, younger travellers find it lacks

ambience and it is certainly less frenetic than Kuta-Legian. There is good diving and you can paddle out to the coral reef, or rent a *prahu*. Mountain-bikes can be hired.

Accommodation

Bali Lovina Beach Cottages, tel: (0362) 41385. New hotel with swimming pool/bar. On the beach. Moderate.

Banyualit Beach Inn, tel: (0362) 41889. Quiet, near the beach, it has clean rooms with large bathrooms and comfortable beds. Indonesian and seafood restaurant. Good value.

Baruna Beach Cottages, tel: (0362) 41252. The first hotel on the right on the road from Singaraja, it is on a delightful site, and has 24 rooms, good food and pleasant staff. Snorkelling and reef trips. Safe for children. Cheap.

Nirwana Cottages, tel: (0362) 41288. On a shady site right on beach. Attractive traditional style cottages, but sloppy service. Cheap.

Food and Drink

Check roadside menus. **Harmoni** restaurant in Anturan and **Khi Khi** restaurant (220 yards/ 200m from Nirwana Cottages) serve good, fresh seafood. The restaurants of **Baruna Beach Cottages** and **Banyualit Beach Inn** are also recommended.

Shopping and Nightlife

Penny Shop is the general store in central Lovina. Nightlife centres on small restaurant/bars.

Travelling On

There is a regular *bemo* service to Singaraja and several daily bus services to Gilimanuk.

◆◆◆
MAS

central Bali, 12 miles (20km) from Denpasar

Attractive wood-carving village on the road to Ubud. Many roadside workshops specialise in masks, including **I B Sutarja** (left side); **Balinese Pop Art** (left side); and for cats – the new fad – **Mass Product KT Astawa**.

Accommodation

Taman Harum Cottages, tel: 88511 ext 569. Situated next to Tantra Gallery, the Balinese style cottages have a view of rice-fields. There are sunken bath-tubs, and the super décor is by a local family of artists. Pool, restaurant/bar. Moderate.

◆◆
MENGWI

central Bali

The 17th-century royal temple complex of Pura Taman Ayun is here in a beautiful setting surrounded by a moat. It was the state temple under a kingdom which ruled at Mengwi until 1891. Entry is through an elaborate gate. Visit the site in conjunction with Sangeh and the sacred 'Monkey Forest', (see page 64).

Try the **Water Palace Restaurant** for lunch.

◆
NEGARA

59 miles (95km) from Denpasar

The largest town on the jungle-clad west coast, its annual highlight is the September/October bullock-races when pairs of decorated bullocks pull chariots around a rice-field (see page 108). To see this colourful and free spectacle, you should leave Denpasar by 06.00 hours, or stay overnight; tours from the main resorts can also be taken. Standard *losmen* line the main street in Negara. All are basic and none has air conditioning.

Competitors in the Negara bullock races ponder their chances

◆
NUSA DUA
*Southeast Coast, 30 minutes'
drive from Sanur.*
The southern peninsula is best
known for the huge, carefully
planned Nusa Dua tourist
complex. It encloses half a
dozen de luxe hotels, white
sand beaches, well manicured
parkland and sports amenities.
There is a contrived Balinese
atmosphere, but excellent
security.

Accommodation
There are no really cheap
rooms available. More
characteristic is: **Nusa Dua
Beach Hotel,** PO Box 1028,
Denpasar (tel: (361) 71210). This
is a huge hotel (450 rooms and
27 suites) set in tropical gardens
and with bars, cocktail lounges
and restaurants. Dress for
dinner. There are evening
cultural shows as well as tennis,
squash, windsurfing and a
jogging track.

Shopping
There are expensive crafts and
clothes shops in the hotels. Art
Market shopping arcade
outside the gate of the hotel
compound. Local village is a
few minutes' walk away, with a
money-changer, general store,
quik-foto, etc.

Nightlife
Each hotel in Nusa Dua has a
programme of good evening
entertainment, (see **Culture**
pages 99-100).

Transport
There are hotel bus services to
Kuta-Legian. Public transport to
Nusa Dua is patchy, but there is
a *bemo* from Denpasar.

*Supplies come by boat from Bali to
Nusa Penida, once a penal colony*

◆◆◆
NUSA PENIDA AND
NUSA LEMBONGAN
These palm-fringed islands are
in the Badung Strait, 1½-2 hours
by motorboat from Padangbai,
Klungkung District. It makes a
fascinating day-trip, or Nusa
Lembongan has rustic
bungalows for a longer stay.
Package-tours depart from
Sanur. Independent travellers
should take a *bemo* to
Padangbai. Large motorboats
leave Padangbai daily from
08.00 hours every hour until
13.00 hours for Sampalan
Mentigi, the islands' port. There
are no facilities on board.

Nusa Penida
The larger of the two islands

(77 square miles/200 sq km), it was a former penal colony for undesirables from the regency of Klungkung. In local mythology, it is the home of the ferocious giant Jero Gede Mecaling, the source of disease, disaster and evil magic. The island has white, powder-sand beaches shaded by coconut palms. The interior is arid and hilly. To walk from the landing to **Sampalan** takes 15 minutes. There are about 50 general stores, a post office and two banks which do not change foreign money, plus one or two crude restaurants. There is little to eat, brackish water and awful dogs.

Things to see on the island include **Pura Ped** and **Pura Batukuning** (to the east) temples and unspoiled villages.

There is a basic government hotel which may be closed.

To reach Nusa Lembongan, catch a *bemo* to Toyapakeh (15 minutes). A pretty Muslim fishing village, it has two cafés. One has a WC and sells cold beer.

Bargain the cost of a motorised *prahu* to Nusa Lembongan with a local fisherman – you leave when the fisherman is ready. The trip takes 40 minutes.

Nusa Lembongan

This small island protected by coral reefs has white sand beaches, surfing and rustic game-fishing in the channel between it and Nusa Penida. There are no cars. You can walk from the landing site to a small village selling day-to-day requirements for the 2,000 inhabitants. Most people cultivate seaweed; at night they work by lamps when the lagoon twinkles like a 'night market'. Get up early to see the gardens at low tide. Laid out to dry, seaweed covers the island like a green carpet. It is sold to Japan, Singapore and France for processing into cosmetics and crackers.

Accommodation

This consists of basic *losmen* and bungalows. Stay on the beach rather than in the village. **Main Ski Inn, Wave Stay** and the **Nusa Lembongan Restaurant/ Bungalows** are recommended. They are simple and airy with exterior WC and showers. Island dress is casual.

Food and Drink

Eating is very limited. You can

Two routes meet at the port of Padangbai: the Lombok car-ferry and the boat to Nusa Penida

get *nasi goreng* and occasional fish at the **Nusa Lembongan Restaurant/Bungalows** and **Johnny's.** Cold soft drinks and beer are available. Take supplies if you plan to stay two or three days. A tourist hotel-restaurant is planned.

◆
PACUNG
central Bali
This small hillside village *en route* to Lake Bratan is recommended for a delightful hotel with comfortable rooms and spectacular views of the rice terraces, the **Pacung Cottages/Bar and Restaurant** (tel. (0361) 3839). It makes an excellent lunch stop; licensed and with a clean WC.
There is a shuttle-bus service to Bedugal, four miles (7km) away.

◆
PADANGBAI
East Coast, about 1¼ hours' drive from Denpasar
This small, scruffy Muslim port has no tourist facilities. It is the departure point for Nusa Penida–Lembongan (see page 60) and the car-ferry to Lombok. If you have an early sailing, stay over-night at the **Puri Buitan Hotel** at Balina Beach, 15 minutes' drive (see page 45). Local reefs offer good diving for experienced divers only.

◆
PEJENG
central Bali, on the Tampaksiring road.
The village is known for the Temple of the Moon – **Pura Penataran Sasih** – housing a vast bronze drum believed to be 1,000 years older than the Kingdom of Pejeng which came to an end in 1343. Legend says it came to earth as a fallen

moon. The largest single cast drum in the world (it is about 10 feet/3m long), the great brass 'Moon Drum' is set high up in a pavilion. You can hardly see it. The **Museum Arkeologi** is just outside Pejeng.

◆◆◆
PELIATAN
Bali heartland, ½ mile (1km) south of Ubud
Flourishing arts and crafts centre with one of the finest *gamelans* in Indonesia. Lots of galleries with industrious young artists. Popular with Westerners wanting to study Indonesian culture. Some *losmen* teach Balinese dancing.
Agung Rai Gallery is a huge art complex of *atap*-roof cottages (*atap* is stripped palm fronds). Each houses a different school of local art. Ask to see the owner's private collection of paintings by European artists. Dances and rehearsals can be seen in the ***bale banjar*** pavilion. Check times. There are Friday evening and Sunday morning rehearsals.

Accommodation
Stay here as an alternative to Ubud.
Homestay Puri Agung, Jalan Peliatan. Clean, quiet, Balinese-style bungalows. Owner teaches dancing. Cheap.
Mudita Inn, Jalan Peliatan. Rooms with or without a bathroom, or *mandi* (see page 123). Family-run with home cooking. Cheap.

Food and Drink and Shopping
Eat at local *losmen* and village *warung*. See **Ubud,** page 74, for restaurant recommendations.

Local paintings are the best buys for souvenir-hunters.

◆◆◆
PENELOKAN
Central Mountains, 4 hours' drive from Denpasar
This is a popular tourist stop on the southern rim of Gunung Batur, at 4,757 feet (1,450m). Enjoyment of spectacular views is spoilt by hasslers. Do not leave your vehicle unattended. The town seethes with tourists and touts from mid-morning until 15.30 hours. To get here, if travelling by *bemo*, change at Gianyar, or Bangli.
You can walk from Penelokan around the crater rim and descend to the caldera and Lake Batur.

Accommodation
Basic *losmen*, which are tolerable on the coast, are miserable at cooler altitudes. Some have a fire – supply your own logs. People in Penelokan-Kintamani are very mercenary and charge what they think you can pay.
Losmen Gunawan hassle-free site on a spur with a great view of the volcano. Ask for an exterior room. Comfortable and friendly. Cheap.

Food and Drink
Tourist-style restaurants cater for coaches. The **Kintamani Restaurant** is expensive, but serves the best food. Freshly grilled Lake Batur perch is on the menu at the **Losmen Gunawan** which is licensed. Plenty of exotic local fruit.

Shopping
You can buy woven goods, textiles and trash.

Travelling On

Main roads pass Bangli and Ubud; there is a rough branch road to Besakih. Onward buses go to Singaraja. Western routes are poorly served by public transport. Trust no-one proffering his services as a mechanic and do not stop for local hitchhikers.

◆◆
PULAKI

North Coast, east of Gilimanuk
The village is visited for its large sea-temple which commemorates the arrival in Bali of the saint-priest Nirartha in the 16th century. The temple is inhabited by monkeys. There is a good view from the top. Villagers sell grapes – the region is cultivated with vines. Hot springs are a feature.

◆
SANGEH

central Bali within walking distance of Ubud
This is the site of the sacred 'Monkey Forest', which the Balinese believe is featured in the Hindu epic, the *Ramayana;* chopping of wood is forbidden. **Pura Bukit Sari** is a forest temple with ferocious guardians. Monkeys and hasslers are a nuisance. Do not take food for the monkeys or encourage them in any way – or it could be the last time you see cameras, sunglasses, etc. Unfortunately the site is a tourist trap. Get there by direct *bemo* service from Denpasar (Wangaya station).

◆◆◆
SANUR

Southeast Coast, 20 minutes' drive from Denpasar
Quieter, safer, more sheltered – and more expensive – than Kuta, this picturesque, palm-lined coast lets tourism and Balinese lifestyles co-exist: the fisherman's wife may work as a masseuse after 10.00 hours.

Monkeys live in the temple at Pulaki, on Bali's north coast

Those fishermen pushing nets up and down the beach are catching tiny 'tropicals' for export to aquariums 'Down Under'. Get up early (06.00 hours) to see Sanur when it is most Balinese – girls taking offerings to the temples and families breakfasting on the beach. By 10.00 hours they are replaced by tourists swimming, para-gliding, windsurfing and riding jet-skis. Behind the beach 'Sanur Beach Street' (Jalan Tanjung Sari) winds south to **Semawang,** a small coastal village at the southern end of Sanur and away from mainstream tourism. With good hotels and shopping, it is highly recommended as a beach base. Local swimming is best when the tide refreshes the lagoon. There is no surf and it is safe for children. At low-tide you can walk out to the reef.

Beach hotels have sports centres. Various co-ops are also run by Balinese beachboys. **Cemara Watersports Centre** at Semawang offers snorkelling, sailing-boat hire and jet-scooter rides. The lagoon is excellent for windsurfing. Para-gliding is popular.

You can visit the home-turned-museum of Le Mayeur, a Belgian artist who lived in Sanur, 1932–58, in Bali Beach Hotel road.
Closed: Monday

Accommodation

There are over 50 hotels between Sanur and Semawang. A booking is advised.
Alit's Beach Bungalows, Jalan Hang Tuah, Sanur (PO Box 102, Denpasar). Tel: (0361) 88567.

A beachboy demonstrates windsurfing at Semawang

100 bungalows set in large, unkempt gardens. Grey-sand beach. Convenient to bowling centre and golf course. Possesses Bali's most hideous statues, urinating in a fish-pond. Moderate – cheap.
La Taverna, Jalan Tanjung Sari, Sanur (PO Box 40, Denpasar). Tel: (0361) 88497. Do not be misled by the name – it consists of 40 pleasant Balinese-style bungalows in gardens behind the beach. Quiet, with excellent Indonesian food. Convenient to shops. Suitable for all travellers. Moderate.
Segara Village, Jalan Tanjung Sari, Sanur (tel: (0361) 88407). At the beach end of a rough lane, these are beautiful cottages in lush gardens. Pool with sunken bar, aviaries, kids' playground. Chinese, Italian, seafood

restaurants. Very popular.
Expensive.

Semawang Beach Inn, Jalan
Cemara Beach, Semawang-
Sanur (tel: (0361) 8619). In quiet
location, 220 yards (200m) from
the beach. Friendly staff, clean
rooms with air conditioning and
private bathroom. Ideal for two
friends sharing and
independent travellers. Bar.
Good value.

Surya Beach Cottages, Jalan
Mertasari, Semawang (tel:
(0361) 88833). Large,
comfortable Balinese-style
cottages set in gardens in
private beach location. Pleasant

*Surya Beach Cottages enjoy the
seclusion of a private beach*

atmosphere – no hustlers.
Facilities include watersports,
tennis, travel agent, baby-sitter.
Ideal for families as well as
couples. Within walking
distance of Semawang village.
Moderate – expensive.

Tourist Beach Inn, Jalan Segara
Ayu, Sanur (tel: (0361) 88418).
Basic rooms; 110 yards/100
metres from the beach. Cheap.

Villa Bebek, corner of Jalan
Pengembak and Jalan
Mertasari, Semawang (PO Box
47, Denpasar). Tel: (0361)
321507. Three villas and one
guest cottage in classic Balinese
style, sharing large swimming
pool. Each villa has its own
entrance, kitchen and dining
pavilion. Gorgeous but
expensive.

Villa Kesumasari II, Jalan
Kesumasari, Semawang-Sanur
(tel: (0361) 88371). Potentially
excellent, but spoiled by
barking dogs. Basic cottages on
the beach with private
bathrooms, air conditioning and
friendly staff. Cheap.

Food and Drink
There are Western-style bars
and restaurants on Jalan
Tanjung Sari. Bali-Indonesian
restaurants are few and far
between.

Jawa Barat, in Semawang, is a
cheap, popular Indonesian
restaurant; licensed with helpful
staff. Menu in Indonesian.

Kesumasari Restaurant, on the
beach at Semawang, serves
simple seafood-style meals.
Licensed with lunch
recommended.

Kulkul Restaurant, central Sanur,
has a good reputation for
seafood and local specialities.

La Taverna Hotel (see above).
Attractive poolside restaurant
with Indonesian buffet and à la
carte western menu.
Tanjung Sari Hotel, central
Sanur, has a seaside bar and a
weekly *rijstaffel.*
Expectations of romantic
dinners on the beach are
spoiled by midges. 'Aussie
breakfasts' are advertised by
many places on Jalan Tanjung
Sari. Most are spoilt by loud
music and an odour of 'bar' from
the night before. Avoid surly
service and mean portions in
'Alit'. Shop No 3 in Sanur Art
Market sells coffee and freshly
baked croissants. You can even
get lax and bagel.

Nightlife
Sanur does not have Kuta's
rowdy nightlife, but Australian
ravers are still found in discos
such as **No 1** and **Sobek.** Life
starts around 23.30 hours. The
Hyatt's **Mata Hari** disco attracts
sophisticates.

Shopping
Most shops in Sanur are a
rip-off, but if you have not
shopped in Mas-Ubud, try **Ucok
Antiques** for primitive art, and
the gallery **Eurasia Bali;** both are
near the Bali Hyatt. There are
bookshops, money-changers
and pharmacies on 'Sanur Beach
Street'.

Tours
Sanur-Semawang is the best
base for sightseeing in Bali.
Shop around for dance-tickets
and tours.
You can take a day-trip to
Serangan Island or 'Turtle
Island', south of Sanur, close to
Benoa harbour. The island looks

charming from the shore, but it
is a tourist trap. If you want to go
there, wait until low-tide when
you can walk out. There is a
turtle nursery with miserable
turtle pens, and a temple, Pura
Sakenan.

◆◆
SINGARAJA
*North Coast, 53 miles (85km)
from Denpasar*
This was the old Dutch capital
and a major port in colonial
times. The present population is
about 16,000. It is now a busy
market town counting many
different religious groups –
Muslim, Chinese, Buddhist and
Hindu. Little Western influence
remains except for vestiges of
19th-century colonial buildings.
You should visit the old **harbour
area** with its monument to
independence, and the **Gedong
Kirtya** at the eastern end of Jalan
Veteran, a historical library with
over 3,000 old Balinese
manuscripts inscribed on *lontar*
palm-leaf.
Open: 08.00 hours Tuesday to
Saturday, but make an
appointment as this is a working
library, not merely a tourist
attraction.
Also worth a look is the market
square, with its rows of Chinese
shops.
Hand-weaving is the local craft,
and you can look into a factory,
just behind the library, to see it
being done.
Another attraction is the bullock
races held after harvest (see
page 108). For details check
with the Tourist Office (tel:
(0362) 21142).

Accommodation
There are hotels in the town,

WHAT TO SEE ON BALI

The old Dutch influence is reflected in the 19th-century architecture of Singaraja, once the colonial capital

mostly on Jalan JA Yani, but it is more pleasant to stay at Lovina (see page 58). Recommended in Singaraja is:
Hotel Duta Karya, 59 Jalan JA Yani (tel: 21467). Convenient to Garuda office and local *bemo* station, it has spotless rooms with private bathrooms. Moderate.

Food and Drink
There are good eating-places around **Pasar Mumbil** market on Jalan JA Yani, and recommended Chinese food at the oddly named **Restaurant Gandhi** (fairly expensive).

Shopping
Best buys are hand-woven sarongs and silverware from the local village of Baratan.

Travelling On
Buses and mini-buses to Denpasar depart half-hourly (06.00-16.00 hours) from Stasion Banyusari. Singaraja is the major transport terminal for the north and buses leave for everywhere, including overland to Java-Surabaya. Ticket offices are at the junction of Jalan JA Yani and Jalan Diponegoro.

◆
SUKAWATI
East Coast 9 miles (15 km) north of Denpasar
In this dirty market town, shops along the main road sell wind-chimes and woven hats, bags, mats, etc. Coach tours stop at the 'Sukawati Art Market' – in a huge, cramped, poorly lit complex selling a lot of trash compared to the well-made artefacts in Mas-Ubud. You get what you pay for.

◆
TABANAN
southwest Bali, en route to Negara, 46 miles (74km) northwest
With Badung and Gianyar, the district of Tabanan forms the island's richest rice-belt.

Tabanan township, like other former capitals, has been overtaken by Denpasar. It has little of interest although it is historically associated with *gamelan* orchestras. Mario, the famous exponent of pre-war classic dance, came from here. **Subak Museum** covers the history of rice cultivation, irrigation and the *subak* (rice-growers' association) system.

Open: daily from 08.00 hrs.
An animal market is held every three days in Kediri, a village near Tabanan. If you have wheels, picturesque side-roads in Tabanan region often end at deserted surfing beaches. The coast here is not developed for tourism.

◆
TAMPAKSIRING
central Bali, 23 miles (37km) from Denpasar

The town is known for the **Tirta Empul** temple where the Pakrisan river bubbles up in ancient baths. An inscription indicates it has been a sacred site since AD962. People travel from all over Bali to bathe in the crystal clear water: Soekarno had a hill-top palace built so he could watch them.

Unfortunately, Tampaksiring has become a major hawker site. To reach the temple, you have to walk down a long path lined with stalls selling everything from hand-crocheted tablecloths to turtle shells. Expensive drinks and snacks are available. Avoid going at weekends.

Getting There
Take a *bemo* from Denpasar

and change at Gianyar. Most tours include Tampaksiring *en route* to Lake Batur. There is parking.

◆◆
TANAH LOT
Southwest Coast, about 1 hour's drive from Denpasar

A detour at Kediri off the west coast road to Gilimanuk, Tanah Lot is Bali's best known sea-temple, commanding equal reverence to the mountain shrines. Like Ulu Watu (see page 76) it is associated with the 16th-century priest Nirartha. Legend says a huge serpent dwells inside one of the shrines, but it is discreetly left undisturbed.

Tanah Lot is built on a honeycombed rock carved by the tides. At low tide, you can cross to the temple, where a priest demands a donation. Like Tampaksiring, Tanah Lot is central to hard-sell commercialism. Again you must run the gauntlet of souvenir stalls and hawkers, on the path down to the sea. The site is especially crowded with tourist buses at sunset. To avoid everyone go on an early morning high tide.

Transport
There is no regular *bemo* service. You can be dropped, but getting back is difficult. There are tours visiting Tanah Lot from Kuta.

◆◆
TENGANAN
East Coast, inland from Candi Dasa

Like Trunyan (see page 71), a Bali Aga village, having

friendlier inhabitants. It is a walled village with a typical town square shaded by a huge banyan tree. Simple restaurants sell snacks and drinks. Tenganan's 180 or so families follow Bali Aga traditions dating from before the Majapahit invasion of Bali. They do not marry outside, and celebrate ancient marriage customs. *Kawin pandan* is a yearly event, when a young man throws a flower over a wall and the girl who catches it (even if she is the ugliest girl in Tenganan) is his bride. At the *Usaba sambah*, (an annual festival in June or July) there are processions and boxing contests between men with their fists wrapped in pandanus leaves. The *gamelan selunding*, a sacred, archaic orchestra, performs in Tenganan once a month. Tenganan is renowned for double-*ikat* cloth, in which warp and weft are dyed separately before the fabric is woven. It has a typically dark terracotta background with white and yellow patterns. The cloths are used in teeth-filing ceremonies, at weddings and to bury the dead. Only about six families still know the old *ikat*-process, and Tenganan is the only place in Indonesia where it is done.

Shopping

Local craft products are double-*ikat* and other woven fabrics, shawls, woven baskets, bamboo musical instruments and palm-leaf books. Check a few different shops and houses for quality, and price.

Getting There

There is a *bemo* from Candi Dasa. It is a detour of about 1¾ miles (3km) uphill (but easy walking) off the main road, south. If you do not want to walk, motorcyclists offer pillion rides up (for a fee). Or you can rent a bicycle in Candi Dasa and freewheel back down.

◆◆◆
TIRTAGANGGA

East Coast, 15 minutes' drive from Candi Dasa

This is one of the best spots to relax in Bali with a tranquil site and walks through stunning rice-terraces. It is known for an Indian-style water palace with statues, fountains, lily-ponds, built in 1947 by the water-loving raja of Ujung (see page 76). There is a clean public swimming pool and a *warung* at the gate. There are no banking facilities, so bring what money you may need – very little is necessary beyond the charge for entry to the water palace.

Accommodation

This is limited to peaceful *losmen*.
Tirta Ayu Home Stay is within the water palace complex. It consists of four clean, basic bungalows, superb for solitary travellers. A pleasant restaurant overlooks the tanks. Good fish. Cheap.

Travelling On

A *bemo* runs into Amlapura. Buses continue on to Singaraja – there is a bus-stop outside the water palace. Hitchhiking up the northeast coast is usually simple as there are far fewer tourists than in other parts of Bali. Hitchhikers tend to be treated more like locals.

TOYA BUNGKAH, see **GUNUNG BATUR**

◆◆◆
TRUNYAN
on Lake Batur
Accessible generally by boat, the village is inhabited exclusively by an ethnic tribe with ancestral links predating the Majapahit invasion. Dark, taciturn folk, the Bali Aga are culturally as well as ethnically different to the Balinese. The dead are not cremated. Wrapped in a shroud, a corpse is left in a bamboo cage. If it has not disappeared within a few weeks, it is unceremoniously tossed into the forest. Skulls, bones and old coins are scattered about the clearing by the lake – 1¾ miles (3km) from

The Trunyan people are a race apart from the Balinese, and have their own customs and practices

the village. Other customs are kept secret. Bali's largest statue of Ratu Gede Pancering – 13 feet (4m) high – guardian of Trunyan, is hidden.
Trunyan is not a place to stay, as there are primitive facilities only in the village. Visit is by donation – be prepared for extravagant demands from the people. Fish-hooks are appreciated.
See also **Tenganan** and **Gunung Batur** (pages 69 and 50).

◆◆
TULAMBEN
on the northeast coastal road
The village is reached via a spectacular drive from Tirtagangga. Terraced rice-fields alternate with barren lava flows and the road skirts the base of Gunung Agung.
People visit Tulamben for the diving off accessible coral reefs.

WHAT TO SEE ON BALI

The wreck of a US Liberty ship, torpedoed in 1942, lies one mile (1.5 km) offshore at a depth of 20-98 feet (6-30m). The *losmen* (see **Accommodation** below) organises diving packages including airport transfers.

Accommodation
Paradise Palm Beach Bungalows, PO Box 31, Amlapura. 10 small, comfortable bungalows on the rocky beach. Friendly atmosphere. Small, licensed restaurant. Unsuitable for young children.

◆◆◆
UBUD
south-central Bali
An hour's drive from the airport and 21 miles (34 km) from Kuta,

Rice fields near Ubud, a haven of tranquillity and centre of culture

Ubud is the perfect foil to 'sun 'n surf'.

With Mas, and surrounding hamlets, Ubud is the cultural heart of Bali. The island's most skilled wood-carvers, painters, musicians, dancers and artists live here. There are schools where you, too, can study dancing and mask-making. Foreign artists such as Rudolf Bonnet and Walter Spies were residents of Ubud between the wars and there is still a small, semi-permanent community of Western artists. Culture apart, Ubud is a base for enchanting walks. There is nowhere like it: do not dismiss it in a few hours' visit.

Sightseeing
At first sight the town centre gives the impression of being a rural Kuta. To an extent this is true, but Ubud manages to strike a balance between nature and commercialism. Money-changers, galleries, souvenir shops – and even a supermarket – line its long, often muddy main street. Signs also advertise bicycles, *barong* dances and cheap tours. In the centre is a temple and tranquil lotus garden. Walk from the post office to Murni's Warung by the Campuhan bridge and back.
Lotus Garden. A lotus-choked pond set in peaceful grounds, it is perfect for contemplation.
Museum Puri Lukisan. From the gardens, cross the river gully and climb the hill to reach Ubud's fine arts museum. Established in 1956, the museum traces the evolution of local art from early masters to the so-called 'young artists', who

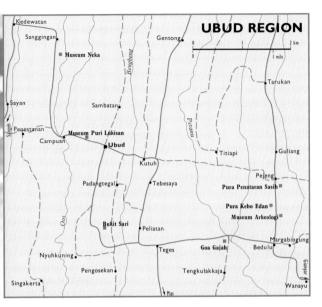

evolved a new style of painting in the 1960s. Museum and gardens are both in need of upkeep.
Open: daily 08.00-16..00 hrs.
Museum Neka. To reach it, turn right beyond the suspension bridge – about 30 minutes' walk. The museum exhibits modern art produced by Balinese and other Indonesian artists, and with works by Western artists who painted in Bali, among them Theo Meier, Donald Friend, Arie Smit and Hans Snel.
Open: daily 08.30-17.00 hrs.

Local Walks
Ubud and its environs is a walker's paradise of deep jungle-clad river gorges and lush rice-fields. Walking is entirely safe. Should you become lost, hit the main road and stop a passing *bemo.* Just 1¾ miles (3km) outside Ubud, the Ananda Cottages are an ideal base (see below under **Accommodation**). Walk from here to Campuhan and Penestanan, one of the main villages of the 'young artists'. You will pass other small hotels hidden in the rice fields.
Wanara Wana (Monkey Forest Road) Walk. This is easy to follow, straight out of central Ubud. It is lined with *losmen* and shops, but further along you enter the cool forest. Be careful of monkeys. You can walk on to Peliatan (see page 63). Be a little cautious of young men lurking along the Monkey Forest Road – this is Ubud's worst area for thieving.
To Pejeng. A trail beyond the

WHAT TO SEE ON BALI

T-junction takes you via a river gorge to Pejeng. *En route* you pass the **Pura Kebo Edan,** or buffalo temple. Balinese humour gives the buffalo statue six penises. For **Pejeng temple,** see page 62.

Bentuyung Walk. This is a loop of about five miles (8 km) through beautiful rural scenery. Return via Kutuh reaching the tarmac near Peliatan. Locals are used to walkers and most understand sufficient English to point you in the right direction.

Accommodation

Ubud counts some of the nicest accommodation in Bali. Hotels and *losmen* are scattered liberally in and around the town. Villages such as Penestanan and Peliatan also have places to stay. The Monkey Forest Road has dozens of cheap homestays. Some hotels are literally planted in the rice fields.

Ananda Cottages, PO Box 205, Denpasar 80001 (Telex: 35428). Five minutes by taxi from Ubud, 35 cottages, plus four family bungalows with kitchen, in a gorgeous location surrounded by rice fields. Ask for nos 16-18. Pool and rural walks. Licensed restaurant, pleasant staff. Moderate.

Cahaya Dewata Country Villas, Kedewatan (tel: 95171). Near the Museum Neka 1¾ miles, (3km) from Ubud – 22 spacious rooms overlooking the Ayung River Valley. Some steep climbs for older guests. Ideal for couples. Pool and licensed restaurant. Western and Indonesian breakfasts – excellent black rice with wine and coconut milk. Very quiet. Courtesy car to

Ubud. Moderate tariff.

Kori Agung Bungalows, PO Box 10, Ubud. In the heart of the rice fields at Campuhan-Ubud. Comfortable and friendly, with a refrigerator in each room, but no hot water. Hard to reach if you have lots of luggage. Great value.

Kupu Kupu Barong. Luxurious 2-storey Balinese bungalows overlooking the Sayan Valley. Pool and licensed restaurant. Up to three children to 16 years may share with two adults. Free bus-service to Ubud. Views better than the food. Expensive.

Murni's Bungalows by the Campuhan bridge. Comfortable, quiet and convenient to central Ubud. Meal service from Murni's Warung (see **Food and Drink** below). Moderate.

Puri Saraswati Bungalows, Jalan Ibu Raka Arimas (tel: (0361) 95164). In central Ubud, next to the Lotus Gardens, with comfortable rooms. You have to get used to the sound of rakes scraping up fallen frangipani. Popular, convenient and moderately-priced.

Wisata Cottages, Campuhan, 1¼ miles (2km) from Ubud – 16 clean, simple cottages overlooking farmland. Swimming, table tennis. No charge for up to two children under 12 with parents. Cheap.

Food and Drink

Market stalls serve cheap food. Ubud has a limited number of restaurants.

Han Snel's Garden Restaurant. Jungle sounds in central Ubud. Very good Indonesian food. Closed Sunday.

Lotus Café, just west of the

Views of the Ayung River Valley are had from the Cahaya Dewata Country Villas, Ubud

bemo station, is a relaxed restaurant overlooking the Lotus Garden. Western-style dishes and snacks – pasta, cheesecake, crêpes, etc – are served. Always crowded. Ideal for families. Licensed.

Murni's Warung, by the Campuhan bridge, has Western and Indonesian food. Very pleasant, very popular, very good value. Licensed. Closed Wednesday.

Suci Inn, on the road opposite Monkey Forest Road, offers good homestyle Balinese meals. Order in advance. Authentic setting with *gamelan* music.

Nightlife
This is not what Ubud is about and remains low-key. Local dance performances are advertised.

Shopping
Ubud has many shops, galleries and a somewhat trashy market. Check out the small shops along the Monkey Forest Road. Good places to look for paintings are on the road to the Museum Neka. Visit other artists' villages before you buy.

W Barwa Painter-Workshop is a large roadside gallery in Peliatan. Many talented artists lived in the Padangtegal area – the late Australian painter Donald Friend worked here. Expect to pay £300-£400 ($500) upwards for anything of merit.

Travelling On
Bali's most popular destination, Ubud is well served by public transport. The *bemo* station is beside the cinema. Bicycles may be hired. There is an onward bus service to Penelokan-Lake Batur and Gianyar-East Coast.

WHAT TO SEE ON BALI

◆◆
UJUNG
East Coast
Within walking distance of
Amlapura is the water palace
built in 1921 by Anak Agung
Anglurah, last ruler of
Karangasem (see also
Tirtagangga, page 70), a place
of crumbling pavilions,
reed-choked moats, and canals.
Walk, or drive, over the hill to a
picturesque Muslim fishing
village with black sand beach,
like Tahiti. The road ends six
miles (10km) further north.
There is no tourist development.
An irregular *bemo* service runs
from Amlapura. Take food and
drink for a swim/picnic.

*The impressive view from Ulu Watu,
famous for boardriding*

◆◆◆
ULU WATU
*southwest coast of Bukit-Nusa
Dua peninsula.*
The Pura Ulu Watu sea-temple
is about 30 minutes' drive from
the Nusa Dua-Kuta road junction
on a badly pot-holed road.
Legend says the Pura Ulu Watu
is a ship turned to stone. It is a
hot climb up to the temple,
dramatically perched on the
edge of a high cliff. Entry, to the
courtyard is forbidden. Be
careful of resident monkeys.
Turquoise surf lashing the cliffs
gives one of Bali's best views.

Surfing
True-blue boardriders surf at
Ulu Watu which has about six
different breaks with a big
swell. 'Inside Corner' and the
'Peak' are most commonly
surfed, but you need
experience. To reach the
beach, take the track marked
'Sulaban Beach' on the right
before Ulu Watu. Several
warung cater to the exclusively
young, bronzed surfing crowd.

◆◆
YEH SANIH
*north coast road, 9 miles (15km)
east of Singaraja*
This is an attractive coastal
centre with freshwater pools
and gardens. **Pura Taman
Manik Mas** temple overlooks
the springs.

Accommodation
Bungalow Puri Sanih. Garden-
style within the springs
complex. Cheap.
Yeh Sanih Seaside Cottages.
Picturesque site overlooking the
ocean. Clean, quiet and
moderately priced.

PEACE AND QUIET

Wildlife and Countryside on Bali and Java

by Paul Sterry

Bali and Java can justifiably claim to be paradise islands. Although Bali in particular has suffered as a result of growing tourism as well as an increase in its own population, both still retain a strange beauty that owes as much to their culture and religion as it does to the landscape.

In these highly populated islands, wildlife and the environment have often had to take second place to the needs of the human population. However, many wonderful wilderness areas of forested volcanic peaks, swamps and coast still remain, full of wildlife. To the credit of the islands, often aided by the World Wide Fund for Nature, some of the best areas are now reserves or national parks.

When the 19th-century naturalist Sir Alfred Wallace visited Indonesia, he noted the unusual geographical affiliations of the region's plants and animals. On islands to the west of Bali, the wildlife is essentially tropical Asian in origin while to the east, the ties are with Australia. In past times, the deep Lombok Straits proved a physical barrier to the spread of plants and animals from west to east. Hence Bali and Java, west of the so-called Wallace Line, have more than twice as many breeding bird species as adjacent Lombok, and a completely different flora.

Bali

Bali is a land of rolling landscapes where everything somehow seems in place. Tradition and religion seemingly pervade the whole of Balinese life. Man's influence not only manifests itself in temples and shrines, but is also strongly felt in the countryside where terraced rice fields are *the* dominant feature, covering most of the southern half of the island.

Yet there is another more natural side to Bali. It is an island of stunning beaches, mangroves, rolling hills and towering, forested mountains. The northern half of the island, dominated by a chain of volcanic peaks, is the region least affected by man, but natural history interest can be found almost anywhere if you look.

The whole of the Indonesian region is dominated by volcanoes, and eruptions – generally on a minor scale – are by no means a rare occurrence. One of the world's most famous volcanoes, Krakatau, lies near by off the west coast of Java. When it erupted in 1883, it killed tens of thousands of people and affected the world's climate. Nowadays, the volcanic peaks of northern Bali are mostly dormant, but one, Gunung Batur, occasionally rumbles and fumes. Intrepid visitors can trek to the summit from Toya Bungkah (see page 51).

The forested slopes of the northern mountains are good for wildlife, if a little difficult to explore. Exotic birds such as

PEACE AND QUIET

A lar gibbon — look out for them in Cibodas National Park, west Java

hornbills, flowerpeckers, minivets, sunbirds and coucals abound and mammals such as leaf monkeys and macaques may also be seen. The further west you travel, the wilder the country becomes.

Closer to Denpasar, the 'Monkey Forest' near Ubud offers close views of tame macaques and attracts large numbers of visitors. Not far from the capital, paddy fields are fished by kingfishers, storks and herons, while edible nest swiftlets hawk overhead for insects. Nearby mangroves are the haunt of crabs and mudskippers, and are feeding grounds for herons and white-browed crakes and waders such as red-necked stints, long-toed stints, Terek sandpipers, wandering tattlers and eastern curlews.

Bali Barat National Park

Bali Barat Taman Nasional lies in the Buleleng district of Bali in the far northwest of the island. The ancient volcanic peaks and dense, tropical monsoon forests which cloak the steep slopes of the reserve are characteristic of much of northern Bali and harbour rich delights for visiting naturalists. Bali Barat lies near Gilimanuk, Bali's westernmost ferry port, and can be reached from Denpasar by travelling along the main western road via Antosari and Negara.

Although Bali Barat is rich in all sorts of wildlife, it is most famous for its Bali starlings, sometimes also called Rothschild's minas. The reserve is their last remaining stronghold and the world population of these beautiful birds is put at no more than a few hundred strong. Part of the reason for their decline is a reduction in suitable breeding habitat, in particular the felling for firewood by local people of the dead acacia trees in which they prefer to nest. The effects of this activity are felt even within the park itself. Fortunately, a nest-box programme may help the starling's plight.

Bali Barat Taman Nasional is best explored early in the morning before temperatures begin to soar and when many of the creatures are at their most active. Colourful butterflies dance in the dappled light along forest rides and paths. Less conspicuous are the park's more retiring inhabitants, such as wild boar, tree shrews, several species of snakes and

banded pittas. Like all members
of this family of birds, banded
pittas are shy and are most
frequently seen either by
chance or by patient and quiet
observation of the undergrowth.
Many of the other birds of Bali
Barat, such as green junglefowl,
coppersmith barbets and pied
imperial pigeons are more
obvious, but flowerpeckers and
sunbirds are so active that they
yield only tantalisingly brief
views.

By way of contrast to the
forests of Bali Barat, the
nearby coasts are well worth
exploring. Mangrove swamps
near Gilimanuk are rich in
fiddler crabs, mudskippers,
herons and kingfishers, while
the marine reserve at Pulau
Menjangan has beautifully clear
water and is good for
snorkelling.

*You need sharp eyes to see leaf
insects like this – after all, they are
designed not to be seen*

Cibodas National Park
Much of the natural jungle
which once cloaked west Java
has long since disappeared,
being replaced by rice fields
and small-scale agriculture. It is
refreshing, therefore, to find
less than 60 miles (100km) from
Jakarta some fine areas of
unspoilt habitat.

Cibodas Taman Nasional
protects wonderful, pristine
areas of rainforest together with
a seemingly endless variety of
plants and animals.

The park's proximity to the
capital means that it can be
visited on a day trip with an
early start. However, to get the
most from the area and in order
to be there at dawn – the best
time of day for views and
observing wildlife – consider
staying overnight. To reach
Cibodas, travel south from
Jakarta to Bogor and then
southeast for about six miles
(10km).

Cibodas National Park was
originally set aside to protect
some of Java's more unusual
forest plants. The Botanic
Gardens, which mark the
entrance to the park, are a
reminder of this. The birdlife is
also good, with most, if not all, of
Java's endemic species being
found, plus numerous insects
and mammals.

Permits and maps can be
obtained from the Forestry
Office in the gardens and to
explore the park properly,
visitors need to be reasonably
fit. The gardens lie at around
4,000 feet (1,220m) and from
here trails lead through the
rainforest past streams, pools
and waterfalls. The ultimate

PEACE AND QUIET

destination is the summit of the volcanic Gunung Gede and *en route* the forest grades into cloud forest and finally low scrub at the highest altitudes. To hike to the summit and back might take 15 hours but it is by no means necessary to undertake this to enjoy the wildlife.

Orchids and other epiphytic plants festoon the trees and tree ferns grow to enormous sizes. Large butterflies fly among the canopies of the immense trees, tree shrews can sometimes be seen and gibbons and long-tailed macaques are often noisy and conspicuous. The birdlife is varied but can be frustratingly difficult to see. The dappled light and dense foliage often conspire to make accurate identification impossible, but azure nuthatch, pygmy tit, black drongo, pink-necked fruit dove and mountain leaf warbler are

Nice bird, shame about the name — this is a black drongo

BALI AND JAVA- WILDLIFE

among the more exotic species that may be encountered.

Ujung Kulon National Park
Lying on the far western tip of Java, Ujung Kulon Taman Nasional is one of the most attractive and unspoilt parts of the whole island. The dense, tropical forest is the main attraction of the reserve but it also boasts marshes and meadows, beautiful waterfalls and stunning beaches and coral reefs. Access and observation is made easy by a network of trails and paths and observation towers and the variety of wildlife to be found in Ujung Kulon is remarkable. Above all else, one creature in particular has made the reserve famous: it is the last haunt of the Javan rhino which undoubtedly would be extinct were it not for this national park.

Although Ujung Kulon is linked to mainland Java by a narrow isthmus, the swampy nature of this land-bridge effectively isolates the park. Access into and out of Ujung Kulon is by

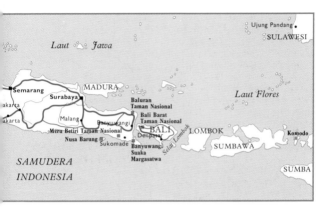

boat from nearby Labuhan where permits can also be obtained from the Forestry Office. Organised tours also operate out of Labuhan which may provide visitors who have a limited amount of time with the best opportunities for seeing the rhinos.

Although people commonly associate rhinos with open grasslands, the preferred habitat of the Javan rhino is the dense jungle where it feeds on leaves and shoots. Males have a single, short horn which is absent in the females. Despite their size, the animals are surprisingly unobtrusive in the forest. They are easier to see when they visit nearby beaches and wallows. Other mammals inhabiting Ujung Kulon are barking deer, sambur, gibbons, wild pigs and wild oxen.

The loud, trumpeting calls of green peafowls herald the dawn, which is undoubtedly the best time of day for walking and birdwatching. Search the forests for ashy drongos, babblers, woodpeckers and flycatchers.

On the beaches you will see waders, terns, herons and kingfishers.

The volcanic island of Krakatau, which erupted in 1883 and devastated the region, lies a short distance to the west of Ujung Kulon. Boat trips can be arranged in Labuhan, about 60 miles (100km from Jakarta), and visitors are constantly struck by the amount of plant and animal life that has colonised the island in such a relatively short time.

East Java

Probably because of the distance from the capital, East Java is more rural than many parts of the island. It can be reached either by a long drive from Jakarta or by ferry from Gilimanuk on Bali. A region of comparatively low and very seasonal rains, east Java has a predominance of plantations, but there are still considerable areas of natural forest left. Almost anywhere that looks unspoilt will harbour wildlife but three areas in particular are especially good: Meru Betiri

Taman Nasional still harbours a few Javan tigers, Baluran Taman Nasional has herds of game animals and Banyuwangi Suaka Margasatwa (Banyuwangi Selatan Reserve) is a remote area of monsoon forest. See map on pages 80-1 for location of reserves.

Meru Betiri Taman Nasional lies on the southern coast of east Java near Sukamade. Hills rise steeply from the sea to an altitude of over 3,000 feet (900m) and these are cloaked in dense forests. Without doubt, the most spectacular plant to be found here is a species of rafflesia, which produces one of the largest but most elusive flowers in the world. Equally spectacular are the reserve's Javan tigers but these are now so rare that visitors are unlikely to see one. Forest birds such as hornbills, jungle-babblers and white-eyes are more easily seen as are the squirrels, long-tailed macaques and leaf monkeys.

Baluran Taman Nasional, in the northeast of Java is an area of monsoon forests, swampy marsh and grassland on the shores of the Bali Straits and overlooked by the volcanic cone of Gunung Baluran. Excellent views can be had of herds of wild oxen, wild pigs, wild dogs (dholes) and sambar deer in the open country. As for birds, marshlands are favoured by stork-billed kingfishers and milky storks, while the forest margins are the haunt of green peafowl, ashy drongos, rufous-winged buzzards and many more.

Banyuwangi Suaka Margasatwa lies on the Blambangan peninsula in the southeast corner of east Java. The comparative inaccessibility of the reserve is the key to the survival of its monsoon forests and pristine beaches. Waders, herons, terns and frigatebirds can seen around the coast, where some of the sandy beaches are visited by nesting turtles. The open forests have leaf monkeys, wild dogs, wild pigs and numerous species of birds.

Rainforests

Rainforests are found throughout the tropics from South America to Africa and from Australia to Southeast Asia. In these regions the rainfall is high, generally over 100 inches (2,540mm) a year and the temperatures are hot, which means the humidity remains constantly high, making an environment suitable for tropical rainforests to thrive. The climate of the rainforests remains largely stable throughout the year although those of Indonesia, being subject to the monsoon rains, have slightly more seasonal variation than rainforest regions elsewhere. With stability comes diversity in the plants and animals. Even the trees are diverse. Unlike areas of temperate forest which comprise maybe three or four species in uniform stands, a good area of primary rainforest (one which has not previously been felled) could be expected to harbour more than 300 species of tree in just a few square kilometres.

Although most parts of Bali and Java are too dry (by tropical

Only a fraction of west Java's once widespread rainforest survives today

standards) for rainforest to grow, much of western Java has a suitable climate. Mountain chains and volcanic peaks elsewhere also provide localised areas of high rainfall suitable for this habitat. One of the first things to strike people as they enter the world of the rainforest is the size and scale of everything. The trees are immense, supported by spreading buttress roots, and give the overall impression of a high, vaulted ceiling. Because little light penetrates the dense leaf canopy high above, many smaller plants choose to grow not at ground level but up in the tree tops. Hundreds of species of orchids and other epiphytic plants grow attached to branches and have aerial roots which never touch the ground. The soils are shallow and low in nutrients, most of what is available being efficiently recycled. Some plants supplement their nutrient intake in unusual ways: pitcher plants catch insects in water traps while the giant rafflesia feeds on the sap of vines.

As elsewhere in the world, Java's rainforests have been largely felled or severely reduced in size although a few areas are protected by national parks or reserves. This destruction is now viewed by many as a tragic loss, not only for future generations but also because of the rainforests' influence on the world's climate.

Monsoon Forest
Bali and the eastern half of Java fall under the seasonal influence of the monsoons, with daily downpours of heavy rain falling from late October until April. For the rest of the year the climate is essentially dry, more so than elsewhere in Java or in Sumatra, Borneo or Malaysia, and it is this seasonal lack of water that has a profound effect on the climate.

With annual rainfalls less than 80 inches (2,000mm) and with such seasonal variation, true

PEACE AND QUIET

rainforest trees cannot survive. Teak and other drought-tolerant species do thrive, however, and give rise to a special type of forest known as monsoon forest. During the dry season, some of the trees lose their leaves and the forest may look dry and lifeless, but with the coming of the monsoons, the foliage becomes lush again, flowers burst into bloom and insect populations flourish.

Search among the foliage and fallen leaf litter and you will soon find an extraordinary variety of insects. Cicadas and bush crickets sing noisily but are often difficult to locate; many of the other creatures are easier to find. Some, like the ants, are small and seemingly everywhere you look, while metallic rhinoceros beetles and giant atlas moths are less numerous but immediately noticeable because of their size. Birdwatching may prove a little more challenging than searching for invertebrates.

An atlas beetle

Although birds of prey, such as crested hawk eagles, may circle overhead, and woodpeckers and drongos feed or perch on exposed branches, other species are more elusive. Forest floor species, such as pittas, thrushes and junglefowl, feed unobtrusively. Early morning walks along quiet trails and paths, preferably on your own or in the company of a few like-minded people, will produce the best sightings. Listen for feeding birds rustling the leaves and creep quietly towards the source of the sound – and you may be lucky. Outside the breeding season, many of the forest's smaller birds roam around in mixed feeding flocks often comprising 20 species or more. Do not be disheartened by an initial apparent lack of birds: at any moment a mixed flock might pass overhead providing the bewildering, if albeit brief, spectacle of several hundred birds.

Blue-tailed banded pitta

Paddy Fields

Rice is probably the single most important crop to be grown on Bali as well as on much of Java. This tropical grass thrives in wetland conditions, and vast areas of paddy cover much of the lowlands, creating a mosaic of flooded fields. Every suitable piece of land is used for rice, as well as some not so suitable areas. Not even hillsides escape the steady march of cultivation: terraces, watered by cunning networks of canals and aqueducts, are a testament to man's ingenuity and a rotation of crop planting allows harvesting throughout the year.

Although the natural vegetation of the region has necessarily been cleared to make way for the rice fields, some wildlife still manages to survive. Frog, insect, and, in some areas, fish populations are high and support large numbers of birds, such as adjutant storks, kingfishers, herons, egrets and birds of prey. From October until March large flocks of migrant waders occur although the species found in them – and their distribution – are rather unpredictable.

Around the Coast

Away from centres of population, visitors to Bali and Java can find beautiful sandy beaches fringed with palms, rocky headlands, coral reefs and estuaries and mangrove swamps, all bathed by the warm waters of the Indian Ocean to the south and the Javan Sea to the north. These are rich in marine life and support thriving populations of both oceanic and coastal birds.

Coral reefs provide a truly astonishing spectacle. Often just a short distance below the surface, colourful corals, anemones and sea fans harbour a myriad of colourful fish, smaller species in shoals and larger fish patrolling territories. Scuba diving is the ultimate way to explore the reef but a simple snorkel and mask is all you really need to enter this world. During periods of onshore winds, particularly along the rougher southern shores, and on ferry crossings, a variety of seabirds may be seen. Sooty and bridled terns are truly oceanic species while crested terns are more frequently encountered closer to shore. Keen-eyed observers may spot Swinhoe's storm petrels, their dark plumage and forked tails aiding identification, or a Christmas Island frigatebird wheeling overhead with its immense wingspan. Where shoals of fish have attracted seabirds, keep a lookout for dolphins and whales which may also be lured by the marine bonanza.

Were it not for disturbance and the regrettable Indonesian liking for their meat and eggs, turtles would nest on sandy beaches all around Bali and Java. Loggerhead, Pacific, Ridley, leatherback, green and hawksbill turtles are now restricted to remote or protected areas such as the Nusa Barung Island reserve off southeast Java, Sukomade Beach in south-west Java or Serangan Island off south Bali. Females, which come ashore at night to lay their leathery eggs in pits excavated in the sand, are cumbersome and vulnerable on land, making them easy prey to local plunderers. Such is the scale and efficiency of the depredations that populations of turtles are under serious threat. Visitors who want to show their disquiet should refuse turtle meat or eggs as well as artefacts made from turtle-shell.

Mangroves
Mangrove swamps grow throughout Indonesia wherever silt-laden rivers meet the sea and form suitable estuaries. Good examples can be seen around Gilimanuk in northwest Bali, near Denpasar and at Baluran in northeast Java. The key element in the formation of mangrove swamps is silt: it must be nutrient-rich and there must be plenty of it. Several species of mangrove can be found in the region but all share a tolerance of saltwater and an ability to grow in choking silt. Their characteristic tangled network of roots encourages the deposition of silt and so the swamps help create new dry land.
Mangrove swamps are incredible places for naturalists. Armies of fiddler crabs, hermit crabs, ghost crabs and amphibious crabs scurry across the surface of the mud at low tide, accompanied by mudskippers, curious fish which spend much of their lives out of water. Some crabs fall victim to crab-eating macaques while several species of kingfishers, egrets and herons also take a toll. Both macaques and herons, as well as human visitors, have

to keep a wary eye open, as the tide rises, for saltwater crocodiles.

Komodo Dragons
Pulau Komodo and neighbouring islands, now a national park, are home to one of the world's most extraordinary creatures, the Komodo dragon. This relict from the age of the dinosaurs thrives on the islands in the absence of competing carnivores and is becoming a major tourist attraction.
To reach Komodo still requires time, effort and money. The island can be reached by island-hopping using ferries and buses which will take several days. Visitors can sometimes join organised tours from Denpasar. Permits to enter the national park should be bought in advance from a Forestry Authority (PPA) office.
Although a dragon in name only, and in reality a species of monitor lizard, the Komodo dragon is no less impressive for it. Adults can reach a length of 6½ feet (2m) and weigh up to 110lbs (50kg) and will kill prey as large as wild buffalo, wild pigs, deer and goats. Despite their ability to tackle live animals, the dragons are lured by the smell of carrion, using a keen sense of smell; visitors, who must always be accompanied by guides from Loho Liang, often use dead goats as a bait. However, if you are offended by the idea of sacrificing a goat, Komodo dragons can usually also be found simply by following their tracks.

FOOD AND DRINK

Indonesian Cuisine

Rice is the staple diet of most people throughout Indonesia. Coconut-milk, hot chillies and spices are common ingredients. Traditional dishes are *gado-gado* (cold vegetable salad with peanut sauce), *soto* (a spicy broth), *saté* (char-grilled meat, poultry or fish) and *nasi goreng* (fried rice usually with vegetables or egg). It is difficult to find fresh fish due to the hot climate and lack of freezing facilities. Tropical fruits are abundant. Beverages are fruit-juices, coffee or tea, rice-wine and excellent beer manufactured under patent to Heineken.

There are many Chinese as well as Western-style restaurants in Jakarta and in the tourist towns on Bali. For recommendations see **Jakarta** pages 30-4 and under individual entries in **What to See in Bali.**

Balinese Food

Balinese food is blander than elsewhere in Indonesia as cooks use fewer spices and chillies. The major difference, however, is that pork, which is anathema to Muslims, is eaten on Bali. Roast suckling pig, or *babi guling* is the island's traditional dish. Duck steamed in a banana leaf, *betutu bebek* is another. The Balinese are also unique in eating turtle, imported from the Moluccas or raised on Serangan Island (see page 67). *Lawar* – raw meat mixed with blood – is also popular. Prepared at home, it is on sale – and eaten – within the hour because of the climate. Country people eat frogs,

Saté *(char-grilled meat or fish) and peanut dip is a hot and spicy Indonesian dish*

worms, snakes, paddy eels, flying-foxes, lizards and dragonflies. Children trap the latter on a wispy pole with a sticky end.

If nothing else, any restaurant patronised by tourists will have *nasi goreng, gado gado* and *saté* on the menu. Common side dishes are cucumber pickle and prawn crackers or *krupek* – delicious when fresh. Fresh seafood is hard to find.

It is in fact difficult to find genuine Balinese food. Your best chance is at a traditional dance and buffet night at one of the international hotels. The **Bali Oberoi** in Legian does an excellent Indonesian buffet with *babi guling.* The genial Balinese chef at **La Taverna Hotel** in

FOOD AND DRINK

Sanur cooks island specialities such as *betutu bebek*. As in Jakarta, although they are not so good, *warung* or street stalls are recommended. Night markets have a mix of Chinese as well as Indonesian food. Common items are *mi-goreng* (fried wheatflour noodles) and *chapchaai* (an elaborate version of chop-suey). One stall will always specialise in *soto nasi goreng* and *nasi campur* (steamed or boiled rice with vegetables, meat or fish). Instead of soya sauce favoured by the Chinese, you get a small dish of *sambal*, a fiery dip made from chillies, dried shrimp paste and lime-juice.

Balinese love snacks. Everywhere are people selling tiny packets of food, rice-cakes and crunchy biscuits. Most things are a mystery: you need an Indonesian-speaking companion to explain. The Central Market in Denpasar is filled with snack-stalls. Try *onde-onde*, delicious sesame-seed studded balls of blue rice with bean paste and palm sugar fillings. You can eat your fill for £1.50 or $2.

Apart from on ceremonial occasions, the Balinese are modest eaters. The two or three daily meals revolve around boiled white rice, with small portions of lightly spiced meat or poultry, vegetables, peanuts and cucumber. There are no set meal times; people eat when they are hungry. Food is cooked in the early morning and left in covered pots on the kitchen table. Eating is normally not communal as members of the family come in at odd times to serve themselves.

Feasts are different. Preparing food for all the relatives at a wedding, or a funeral, may take all night until morning. The men gather to prepare *lawar*, and the suckling pigs. When preparations are complete, portions are divided on banana-leaf 'plates' for offering to the gods before everyone eats. The gods are fed every day. If you are up early, you will see young girls quietly leaving tiny trays outside the shrines. Those placed on the ground are devoured by dogs. The Balinese eat with their right hand, taking a lump of rice, dipping it in *sambal* and inserting in the mouth with the thumb. Water is commonly drunk with a meal.

Balinese Beverages

Tea *(teh)* is popular. Fragrant, like Chinese tea, it is drunk hot, or cold, with sugar *(manis)* or without *(pahit)*. Coffee is rarely well made. Strong, it has lots of grounds floating. Black coffee is *kopi Bali* and white, *kopi susu*. **Made's Warung** in Kuta (see page 56), knows how to prepare good espresso-style coffee. Alcoholic beverages include *brem* (rice-wine), *arak* (distilled rice brandy), and *tuak* (sweet palm-beer). Old *brem (brem tua)* is more expensive; drinking too much may give you a headache. Local bottled 'Ankor' and 'Bintang' are pleasant, light lager with a lower alcohol content than Western beer. Outside tourist-resorts it is hard to find cold beer. Beer *pakai es* (with ice) is proffered, but best refused. Familiar Western soft drinks are readily available; but

try the Balinese bottled drinks like *Temulawak*, a spicy, fizzy concoction. Bottled mineral water is also available.
Fresh fruit-juices are very popular thirst-quenchers in Bali; they are also sold in cartons. *Jeruk* is the general name for citrus fruit; *air jeruk* (orange juice) and *air jeruk nipis* (lemon juice) may be sold hot, or cold. Cool juices are made from pineapple, mango, apple, papaya, passionfruit, banana, litchi and other fruits. There is a drinks stand outside every market. Some of the beverages are exotic concoctions like *es kopyor*, made from rose syrup, ice and tender lumps of coconut jelly. Equally delicious is *es campur*, a blend of jelly, fruit and shaved ice. Beware of anything made with ice unfortunately.

A treat for the eye and the appetite: exotic Balinese fruits

Fruits

Bali grows an abundance of tropical fruits; familiar types such as bananas, plus exotic species like *salak*, a heart-shaped apple covered in snake-like skin. You should try the following – all are sold in Denpasar, depending on the season.

Blimbing: starfruit or carambola – cool, crisp, yellow fruit which resembles a star when cut.

Durian: huge, greenish-yellow spiky fruit greatly revered by locals. Smells like rotten cheese; tastes like creamy banana custard.

Mangosteen: about the size of a billiard ball, with smooth purple skin which stains your fingers. The green segments on top are said to resemble, exactly, the luscious white lobes within. Balinese bet on how many lobes there will be, from one to eight. Slightly tart taste of litchi and passionfruit.

Nangcur: or jackfruit – the largest fruit in the world – may weigh up to 44lbs (20 kilos). Knobbly yellowish-green skin. Bright yellow, slightly rubbery segments.

Passionfruit: if you think you know passionfruit, wait until you see the huge, yellow-skinned passionfruit grown around Kintamani. Milder tasting than familiar purple varieties.

Rambutan: round, hairy greenish-red fruit. Sweet, soft, translucent flesh, with a taste similar to litchi.

Salak: or snake-fruit. Peculiar apple-textured fruit. Grows around Rendang, and slopes of Gunung Agung.

Zuzat: or custard apple. Warty blackish-green skin covering slightly tart segments. Best eaten when slightly soft.

SHOPPING

Bali is a treasure-house of unusual arts and crafts objects. Everyone on the island seems to be creative. In some villages entire families are painters and sculptors. Their talents are natural and they have loads of time. Except for weavers, artists are generally male. Previously they used to paint and sculpt for enjoyment; the tourist market now provides an income. Unfortunately tourism, or what Balinese perceive to be foreign taste, is also flooding the shops with trash, and cheap souvenirs are thrust at visitors to every tourist attraction.

For anyone interested in acquiring something of integrity and quality, here is a brief guide to Balinese arts and crafts.

Painting

With stone-carving, painting is the most exuberant talent exhibited in Bali. Isolated from outside influence, island artists originally portrayed narrative themes from Hindu mythology; bizarre creatures frolicked and fought against a Rousseau-type backdrop of jungle foliage, covering every inch of space. This infinite artistic energy was channelled into three types of painting: large, decorative works for palaces and temples; temple scrolls; and astrological calendars. Paintings were executed in narrative panels with the characters shown in profile. Vivid examples of this style can be seen in Klungkung (see page 54).

Painting changed when Western artists Walter Spies and Rudolf Bonnet came to Bali in the 1930s. Influenced by their work, local artists switched to realism. Scenes of everyday rural life, temple processions and dances became the subject of single pictures. The new trend caught on in the lively arts centres of Mas-Ubud. Political upheaval in the mid-1960s threw many artists into despair but spirits revived with encouragement from Dutch artist Arie Smit. He taught European methods, leaving the choice of subject and composition to the native artists. This new genre of painting known as the 'young artists' developed in Penestan, near Ubud. Busy and colourful is one description of the 'young artist' school.

In truth it is hard to find a contemporary work that pleases enough to buy. Much of the market is happy to have a 'Bali original' without caring about its merits. Galleries are chock-a-block with gharish Bayswater-style paintings, one like the next. If you wish to buy, be guided by early works in museums such as the Puri Lukisan in Ubud (see page 72).

Woodcarving

Balinese are some of the most skilled woodcarvers in Indonesia. Spectacular carvings are everywhere you look: doors, temple struts, free-standing statues and domestic objects. Wood-carving was originally done only for royalty and high-caste families.
Changes from traditional styles began in the 1930s. At first they were subtle – the elongated female torso is an example – but new art-forms emerged. Encouraged by commercial interest, woodcarvers scaled down their sculpture. Small figures and scenes from ordinary life replaced creatures from the ancient epics. Realism became a theme in wood-carving communities in Mas-Ubud. Some celebrated sculptors such as Ida Bagus Tilem of Mas continue to carve abstract representations of the human figure, but influenced by tourist taste; others have turned to pop art. Frogs, birds, pigs and familiar objects are depicted with humour and occasional vulgarity. Carved wooden phalluses are a sign of the times. And, strangely for an island where cats are rare, feline ornaments are hugely popular. Some workshops in

An example of the artistry of Bali's woodcarvers, this stunning mask was produced in Mas

Mas specialise in cats – highly exaggerated, decoratively painted cats – hundreds of them.
Ebony from Sulawesi is the usual choice for classic pieces. It has a fine grain and, when polished, a rich, dark lustre. Some dealers try to cheat by selling local woods like *sawo* and *bentawas*. They are similar, but ebony is heavier. It is also more expensive – about triple the price. Like all master artists, the Balinese produce their share of fakes usually temple artefacts which they call antiques. Attractive, inexpensive carvings feature popular fruits so genuine you could bite them.

Transitory Art-forms

The purest and oldest form of Balinese art is *lamaks*. You can never be tricked into buying an antique, as a *lamak* only lasts a day. They are woven from palm leaf and bamboo folded in hundreds of different ways. You will see them hanging in the temple during a festival. Other perishable art-forms include the spectacular temple offerings made by women, and the giant sarcophagi which go up in smoke on a funeral pyre.

Silverwork

Filigreework made by silversmiths in Celuk and elsewhere has ancient Indian origins: you see similar designs in downtown Delhi. Spinning methods remain primitive and apprentices begin young; some are expert by their teens. Hawkers flogging silver jewellery are a nuisance in Kuta-Legian. Telling them you only like gold is a deterrent. Silver ceremonial daggers, or *kris*, are an interesting proposition. A man's economic status was judged by the richly embellished handle, or sheath. Making a *kris* is time-consuming and they are therefore expensive. Old ones are rarely offered for sale, being family heirlooms.

Weaving

Weaving remains part of a traditional Balinese woman's upbringing. Fabrics vary from simple homespun cotton *sarong* to rich *songket* cloth worked with gold and silver thread. The districts of Klungkung and Karasem are renowned for silk brocade. Bali is also one of the few remaining centres making *ikat*, a time-consuming process, involving dyeing each thread prior to weaving a pattern. As with purchasing a fine Persian carpet, a little knowledge of *ikat* is useful if you intend to buy fabric. (See **Tenganan,** page 70). *Sarong* vary in price. They may cost ten times more than normal at a temple festival.

Other Crafts

Hand-painted kites, wind-chimes, shell objects and basketware are other eye-catching crafts. What is inexpensive, however, may not be a bargain. For instance, a cheap raffish hat will have been woven with green straw and will therefore quickly lose its shape.
Craftsmen also make shadow puppets *(wayang kulit)* and delicate, lace-like fans from buffalo hide. A list of all Bali's hand-crafted goods is endless; it is essential to buy carefully and bargain for anything you fancy.

Bargaining

Most Western travellers feel uncomfortable bargaining, but it is traditional in Asia and should be regarded as a challenge. It can be good fun as well as saving you money. Try to slash at least 25 per cent off the first price.
If you do not want to haggle, shop at Sanagraha Kriya Asta, the government handicraft centre on the Tohpati Road, north of Sanur (see **Denpasar** page 48).

For information on shopping in Jakarta, see pages 34 – 36.

ACCOMMODATION

Bali has a variety of accommodation ranging from basic *losmen* to de luxe hotels. *Losmen* are small cheap inns which often follow the pattern of a Balinese home. This means that, although you have your own bedroom, you spend much of the time communally in the inner garden with the family and other guests – a great way to meet people and experience something of Balinese everyday life. There is even more sharing in homestays, which are licensed private homes. Tariffs for accommodation are quoted in Indonesian *rupiah* or US dollars. A 15.5 per cent tax and service charge is billed by large hotels. *Losmen* and homestays charge a flat rate, often negotiable, and expect cash.

At time of writing, the amount you can expect to pay per night for accommodation, and what you will get for your money, is as follows:

Cheap: Rp 6,000-20,000. Basic, usually clean. Often shared facilities, WC.

Moderate: Rp 25,000-50,000. A clean, usually comfortable room with private bathroom. Excellent value in some cases with traditional Balinese décor and superb views. Likely to have a restaurant/bar and offer most hotel facilities on a modest scale.

Expensive: upwards of Rp 60,000-100,000. Clean, and with professional management. All facilities including swimming pool and shop. Credit cards accepted. Will be used by package tours.

Very expensive: prices are quoted in dollars only, upwards of $100. International standard hotel which would be double the price elsewhere in Southeast Asia and triple the price in Europe.

The massive 62-acre (13-hectare) complex of the Jakarta Hilton

Choosing Where to Stay

Where possible book in advance. If you do not hold a reservation, check in at the hotel desk at Denpasar Airport. Hotel representatives wait outside. Choose a familiar name on your first night, then change to somewhere cheaper. *Losmen* are two a penny in places like Kuta-Legian. Visit half a dozen, or more, until you find one you like. Ask to see the room and bathroom. This is acceptable practice throughout Indonesia. Most are safe, but do not flaunt your valuables; use safe-deposit facilities for spare cash, etc. Some homestays treat you like a member of the family.

In busy tourist periods, bookings are essential in Sanur and Ubud. Ubud has the best moderately priced accommodation in Bali: standards are often extremely high for a modest Rp 35,000. For recommended accommodation in **Jakarta,** see pages 28 – 29.

All hotels recommended in this book were personally checked, but no responsibility is taken for subsequent changes.

CULTURE AND ENTERTAINMENT

The performing arts on Bali are very much interlinked, with dances being dramatic enactments of mythological events to musical accompaniment. Most visitors will attend a performance of some kind during their stay; despite their strangeness to Western ears and eyes, Balinese music and dance can be greatly enjoyed.

Balinese music is best represented by the ancient form of gamelan

Music

There are many musical forms in Indonesia, but the most widespread and highly developed is the *gamelan*. So central is it that the entire orchestra is known as a *gamelan*. It reaches perfection on the islands of Bali and Java. The rippling chords of the *gamelan* are to Bali what the bagpipes are to Scotland, and you will hear it everywhere. Almost entirely percussion, a full *gamelan* orchestra may consist of as many as 80 individual instruments, divided into two separate, but complementary sets. Each is tuned to a different scale. Indeed, no two *gamelans* are tuned identically. These sets of drums, xylophones, metallophones (like a

xylophone, but made from metal), gongs, lutes and flutes are an ancient Indonesian musical form believed to pre-date Hindu culture. They may have their origins as far back as 300BC, when bronze was first introduced to Indonesia from the Asian mainland.

The *gamelan* is played either on its own, or to accompany dance, or puppet theatre *(wayang kulit)*. What you hear are several layers of sound at once: the scale (or 'mode') reflects the mood of the story; for instance the five-tone *slendro* scale reflects cheerfulness, action and festivity, while the seven-tone *pelog* is more solemn. Basically the instruments of the *gamelan* orchestra are everywhere the same, but there are unmistakable differences in the music of the various areas. Ancient forms such as *gong*

selunding are played by the Bali Aga in Tenganan, and Bali as a whole has the greatest variety of *gamelan* tradition in all Indonesia.

Gamelan music is an exclusively male occupation; scores are learned by heart and passed down from father to son. Village *gamelans* are organised through the *banjar* (village committee) and there is great competition between communities. In Sanur and Penestan you will hear the locals practising in the early evening. Mysterious and melodious, like moonlight and flowing water, *gamelan*, once heard, is never forgotten.

Dance
Music and dance are inseparable from religion in Bali. Music accompanies processions, induces trances and welcomes gods to the temples. There are bumblebee dances, frog dances, war dances, dances for choosing a mate, dances to exorcise evil and long, lavishly costumed ballets based on Hindu epics such as the *Ramayana*.

An indelible image of Bali is of the tiny, quivering dancer, wide-eyed, frangipani in her hair, performing stylish and subtly complex movements in a temple courtyard. Dancers and puppeteers, as well as musicians, are trained from an early age. Children as young as three may perform in public. Dancing, like music, is performed in many public places. Everywhere is a potential stage – in a village square, temple courtyard or even a road in front of a temple.

CULTURE AND ENTERTAINMENT

A bamboo pavilion is quickly constructed, a curtain backdrop hung, the *gamelan* arrives, and the dance begins.

While most dances appear dramatic, at heart they are fun. And most important, they are accessible. They take place everywhere, every day, all over the island, especially on the evening of a temple festival. Dancers are almost always ordinary folk, albeit highly expert, who perform in their spare time as we might play squash. If you are early for a *kechak* performance in the Arts Centre in Denpasar, you will see the dancers ferried in by truck.

Tourist demand has had the effect of lowering the standard of dancing in some areas. Mass-produced *barong* and other dances performed daily in the Ubud area do not have a good reputation. Shop around; there are plenty of touts selling tickets. (See page 98 for where you can see performances.)

◆◆Barong

Rivalling *kechak* as Bali's most popular dance, the *barong* depicts the traditional battle between Good – the *barong* – and Evil – Rangda. The *barong* is a mythical beast – half lion, half shaggy dog – propelled rather like a pantomime horse by men inside the elaborate costume. Ferocious-looking, he is nevertheless mischievous and good-humoured. Rangda is a thoroughly wicked witch.

The most usual form of the dance is *Barong Keket*. It begins when the *barong* bounces in and snaps his jaws at the *gamelan*. Rangda then appears, fangs protruding from her mouth, entrails draped about her neck, and the two fight a magical duel. When the *barong* appears to falter, his supporters, wielding *kris* (daggers), attack Rangda. Her power forces them instead to stab themselves, but the *barong* casts a spell which prevents the daggers from piercing their skin. To perform the *barong* properly, the *kris* wielders must be in a trance. After the performance, the temple priest recites appropriate mantras and sprinkles their faces with holy water to bring them round. In addition, a chicken is killed and its blood sprinkled on the ground as a sacrifice.

It is a very colourful spectacle; young children may be frightened in the front rows.

◆◆◆Kechak

Dubbed the 'Monkey Dance', this is the most distinctive and exciting dance on Bali, though it can become tedious. Instead of a *gamelan*, a male choir chants a 'chak-chak-chak' noise (like a monkey chattering). Throughout the dance, which re-enacts an episode from the *Ramayana*, the circle of bare-chested men provide this eerie accompaniment. It rises and falls in accordance with the action, as Prince Rama, Sita, Rawana and Hanuman – the white monkey-god – fight it out.

◆◆◆Legong

Characterised by elaborate, jewelled costumes, exaggerated make-up and highly stylised movements, *legong* is the most graceful of

Balinese dances. There are various forms, but *Legong Kratan* (or 'Legong of the Palace') is the most usual. It features only three dancers – two young girls often only eight or nine years old, and a teenage attendant. The theme concerns the kidnapping of a maiden by the king, Rangkesari, and his preparations for battle. The dance is fragile and melancholic: Peliatan is noted for an outstanding *legong* troupe.

◆◆Ramayana Ballet
This is a lavishly costumed portrayal of the great Hindu epic; also popular in Java. The basis of many Balinese dances, the theme follows the same story as the *kechak:* conflict between Good and Evil. Hanuman, the monkey-god, eventually rescues Sita who is held hostage in Langka (Sri Lanka). The Nusa Dua Hotel performance is very accomplished.

Other Dances
◆**Baris.** In this warrior dance, a young, noble warrior tries out his stance and tactics in a sequence of stylised gestures. The mask-like facial expression is animated only by exaggerated eye movements.

◆**Barong Landung.** Giant, masked puppets give street performances. The terrifying male puppet, Ratu Gede Mecaling, comes from the island of Nusa Penida.

◆**Gambuh.** This is the oldest dance on Bali, perhaps over 1,000 years old, everything from ballet to pantomime. Other dances are descended from it.

Balinese dancers entertain at the luxurious Oberoi Hotel, Legian

◆**Joged Bung Bung.** A flirting dance with audience participation. Girl dancers choose a partner from the audience by tapping him with their fan.

◆**Jauk.** A solo, masked dance requiring great expertise. Since facial expression is concealed, movements must tell all. *Jauk* dancers are great imitators therefore.

◆**Kebyar Terompung.** A male solo dance like the *baris* with emphasis on the creativity of individual talents. The dance was developed by Mario of Tabanan, the famous 20th-century Balinese choreographer.

◆◆**Oleg Tambulilingan** – the 'Bumblebee Dance'. Flirtatious dance, conceived by Mario in the 1950s. It portrays two bees, one male, one female, in search of nectar in a garden.

CULTURE AND ENTERTAINMENT

◆**Pendet.** A slow dance around the shrine when women bring offerings at a temple festival. The basic female dance, a popular opener for dance performances.

◆◆◆**Sanghyang Trance Dances.** The Sanghyang is a divine spirit which enters the body of a young dancer. In the *Sanghyang dedari* two pre-pubescent girls dance a dream-like version of the *legong*. Eyes shut, toes gripping the shoulders of young boys, and apparantly unaware of one another, they perform a perfectly synchronised dance, swaying out at alarming angles. When the choir stops chanting, they slump to the ground. A priest brings them out of their trance by invocations and smashing water jars. Very secretive, the *Sanghyang* is occasionally performed in Kintamani. See it if at all possible, but beware of far from genuine 'trance dances' offered by tour operators.

◆**Tek Tekan Sutasoma.** Panyembrama dance ritual symbolising the joyful reception of gods attending a temple festival.

◆**Topeng.** A masked dance, in which the dancer has to imitate a person – king, minister, or other legendary figure.

Wayang

An ancient art-form, *wayang* or puppet theatre is ever popular. *Wayang kulit* or shadow theatre is famous in Bali. Common themes are drawn from the *Ramayana* or *Mahabharata* epics, although it is supposed to pre-date Hindu culture. The puppeteer, or *dalang* manipulates the puppets behind a lighted screen. It is a one-man show, and he knows several hours of dialogue by heart, using a different voice for each character. Grotesque, but greatly loved by the audience, the puppets are made from buffalo hide (*wayang kulit* is literally 'leather puppet'). Some hotels in Kuta-Sanur stage *wayang kulit*, though you may have a better chance to see it in the countryside. Always ask your hotel or *losmen* if there is going to be a performance while you are there.

Entertainment Venues

Dance and Theatre

Barong Dance: Batubulan Village, every day 09.30-10.30 hrs; Br. Abasan, Singapadu, every day 09.30-10.30 hrs; Puri Saren, Ubud, every Friday, 18.30-19.30 hrs.

Kechak Dance: Ayodya Pura Stage, Tanjung Bungkak, Denpasar, 18.00-19.00 hrs nightly; Art Centre Denpasar, every day 18.30-19.30 hrs; Br. Buni Kuta, every Sunday 20.00 hrs; Padang Tegal, Ubud, every Sunday 18.00-19.00 hrs.

Kechak and Fire Dance: Bona Kangin, Gianyar, every Monday Wednesday, Friday, 19.00-20.30 hrs; Bonasari, Gianyar, every Monday, Wednesday, Friday, Sunday, 19.00-20.30 hrs.

Legong Dance: Peliatan every Friday 18.30-19.30 hrs; Pura Dalem Puri, Peliatan, every Saturday, 18.30-19.30 hrs; Puri Peliatan, Ubud, every Sunday

9.30-21.00 hrs; Puri Saren,
Jbud, every Monday 19.30-21.00
Irs; Br. Tegal, Kuta, every
Tuesday, Saturday, 20.00 hrs.

Shadow Puppet Show: Mars
Hotel, Sanur (tel: 88236), every
Tuesday, Thursday, Sunday,
8.00-21.00 hrs; Oka Kartini,
Tebesaya Peliatan, every
Sunday, 20.00-21.00 hrs.

Tek Tekan Dance: Puri Anyar,
Kerambitan, Tabanan. Times on
request.

Mahabharata: Br. Teges,
Peliatan, every Tuesday,
8.30-20.00 hrs.

Frog Dance: Penjor Restaurant,
Sanur, every Sunday, 19.00 hrs.

Parwa Ramayana: Hotel Menara,
Jbud, every Tuesday,
Wednesday, 20.00 hrs.

The kechak dance is performed to a
vocal accompaniment intended to
suggest the chattering of monkeys

Hotel Entertainment

Many of the hotels in the main
resorts of Kuta, Sanur and Nusa
Dua lay on entertainment of
various sorts. Below is a guide
to some of the treats on offer.

Music

Hotel Bali Beach, Sanur: 'Bali Hai
Supper Club' – international,
nightly 21.30 hrs Monday to
Saturday.
Nusa Dua Beach Hotel: near the
car park-poolside, *Angklung-
gamelan,* Wednesday from
19.30 hrs.
Hotel Melia Bali Sol, Nusa Dua:
Music Room – *Laserdisc
Karaoke*, nightly 21.00-midnight.
Piano bar nightly from 20.00 hrs.
Pertamina Cottages, Kuta Beach:
poolside Hawaiian music with
barbecue from 19.00 hrs
Saturday. Country music
Monday from 19.00 hrs.
Sahid Bali Seaside Hotel: pool
terrace – band and international
buffet, Sunday from 19.30 hrs.
Oriental buffet, Wednesday
from 19.30 hrs.

Traditional Dance

Hotel Bali Beach, Sanur: *Legong*, Monday from 19.00hrs.

Hotel Bali Hyatt, Sanur: *Pasar Malam* (Night Market) with Frog Dance, Monday from 19.30 hrs. *Ramayana* Ballet with *rijstaffel*, Wednesday from 19.30 hrs.

Hotel Sanur Beach, Sanur: *Legong* dance/buffet, Monday from 19.30 hrs. *Ramayana* Ballet/buffet, Tuesday from 19.30 hrs.

Nusa Dua Beach Hotel: *Ramayana*/buffet, Monday from 19.00 hrs. *Legong*/buffet, Friday from 19.00 hrs.

Hotel Melia Bali Sol, Nusa Dua: *Legong*/international buffet, Tuesday from 19.30 hrs. *Kechak*/barbecue, Saturday from 19.30 hrs. Puppet Theatre, Wednesday from 18.30 hrs.

Hotel Putra Bali, Nusa Dua: *Ramayana* Ballet/seafood buffet, Monday from 19.30 hrs. *Legong*/suckling pig, Thursday from 19.30 hrs. *Barong*, Friday from 19.30 hrs. Frog Dance/barbecue, Saturday from 20.00 hrs.

Pertamina Cottages, Kuta Beach: *Legong*, Sunday from 19.00 hrs. Frog Dance, Wednesday from 19.00 hrs. *Ramayana* Ballet, Friday from 19.00 hrs.

Sahid Bali Seaside Hotel: *Legong*/barbecue, Monday from 19.30 hrs. *Ramayana* Ballet, Thursday from 19.30 hrs.

Bali Oberoi Hotel, Legian Beach: *Angklung-gamelan*, Monday; *Legong*/seafood, Tuesday; *Pasar Malam* and *Ramayana* Ballet, Thursday; *Rajapala*/barbecue, Saturday: *Kechak/rijstaffel*, Saturday; Indonesian poolside buffet/cultural show, Sunday. Usual start-time 18.30 hrs.

WEATHER AND WHEN TO GO

Indonesia as a whole has an equatorial climate tempered by trade winds. There are two seasons: dry (between April and October) and wet (from November to March). The

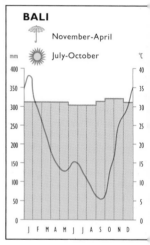

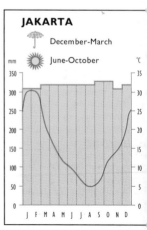

*The tropical rains descend on
Taman Mini bird park, Jakarta*

average annual temperature is
27°C (80°F) in the lowlands and
about 22°C (71°F) in elevated
areas.
Bali has a generally agreeable
climate except before the
monsoon season when it is
unpleasantly hot with humidity
of 95 per cent. Tropical
downpours alternate with
sunshine during the wet season
from October to March
(particularly bad in late
January/early February). Sunny
days with moderate humidity
occur from May to September,
the best time to visit Bali.
Average coastal temperature
varies from about 28°C (82°F)
from May to July to about 30°C
(86°F) in March and October.
Within 1½ hours' drive of the
coast, highland temperatures
are cooler – 16-28°C (61-82°F).
Prospective visitors from the
northern hemisphere should
note that Bali is very popular
with Australians, and Christmas

is a particularly busy time. The
low season is January to May,
and this is the time to go to
avoid the crowds.

HOW TO BE A LOCAL

You are never going to be
mistaken for a native on Bali, but
some knowledge of social
customs and etiquette may
prevent the visitor from
appearing totally insensitive to
Balinese ways.

Everyday Life
Every stage of Balinese life is
marked by ceremony of one
sort or another.

Birth
Balinese adore children and
have plenty to prove it. At the
third month of pregnancy,
offerings are made to ensure
the well-being of the foetus.
After the birth, the placenta is
buried with suitable offerings
and 12 days later the mother is
purified in a cleansing
ceremony. When the baby is
210 days old, its feet are

allowed to touch the ground for the first time, and it is officially welcomed into the family. Twins of different sexes are a catastrophe as they are believed to have committed incest in the womb. Costly ceremonies must be held to purify everyone in the household.

There are only four first names on Bali. Children are named according to the order in which they are born. The first child is Wayan, second Made, third Nyoman and fourth, Ketut. Fifth to eighth are the same again. First-born boys are also known as Gede; Putu is the name of the first-born girl.

Only when a Balinese baby is 210 days old do its feet touch the ground for the first time

Marriage
Balinese marry young. Marriages are not arranged, but they must relate to caste (see next page). Elopement is cheap and appeals to the Balinese fun-loving nature. When the lovers emerge from hiding, their marriage is officially recognised by the families.

Death and Cremation see page 14.

Sexual Roles
Balinese have few social hang-ups. The sexes mix freely but roles are strictly spelled out. Women work much harder. As well as being responsible for running the household, they also buy and sell: 90 per cent of market traders are women. Women also make daily offerings to the temple. What do the men do? They till the fields and plant the rice and while the rice is growing, they do very little. They spend hours talking to friends and preening their fighting cocks. Artistic skills are almost exclusively male-oriented, although both sexes perform traditional dances.

The Home
A traditional Balinese house is surrounded by a high wall enclosing a garden with specific buildings for cooking, ablutions and sleeping. The living room is an open pavilion shaded by a tree, because in the hot climate people tend to live outdoors. Only Western-type homes in Denpasar-Sanur have air conditioning. The actual gateway into the house is staggered to prevent evil spirits simply scooting in. Animals –

dogs, the huge sway-backed pigs and chickens – share the domestic compound.

Village Life

Each adult male joins the village committee – the *banjar* – when he marries. The *banjar* is responsible for decision making: the date of the next cockfight, the hour for *gamelan* practice, etc. Meetings are held in a dirt square shaded by a huge banyan tree. At the main intersection in the village, this is the centre of community life. The village market is also found here, but the *banjar* is an all-male club.

Caste

Like India, Bali has a caste system. Though less strict, it dictates social etiquette, in particular how Balinese address each other. The working class, or village peasants *(Sudras)* constitute the lowest rank. Nobility is divided into three castes. *Brahmans* are the highest caste (only a Brahman may become a high priest); men may have the title *Ida Bagus*. The *Satrias* have the honorific titles of *Anak Agung, Dewa* and *Cokorda*, and the *Vaishyas* are former rulers of local principalities with the title *Gusti*. The Bali Aga are casteless, but there are no untouchables.

Etiquette demands one must be addressed according to one's caste. Hence a Sudra will address a Brahman in a higher form of Balinese. The person of higher caste will respond using 'village Balinese'. There is also a 'middle Balinese', used when caste is not involved. As

well as speaking Balinese, people also speak *Bahasa Indonesia*. Adept linguists, many young people – specifically those associated with tourism – speak English, German or Italian. Bright sparks are also learning Japanese.

Social Etiquette

Social etiquette plays a major part in Balinese life. Respecting traditional ways is appreciated: breaking religious and social taboos may cause offence. It is rude to point with your foot at someone. For those who do not know each other well, touching the other's head is impolite. You are welcome to watch most ritual ceremonies provided you are properly dressed. The unfortunate Balinese are accustomed to scantily dressed Australians, but do wear something decent to visit the temples. Do not stand where the priest will appear smaller than you are and never walk in front of people who are praying. Women may not enter a temple during their menstruation. Notices outside temples advise women of this requirement. A temple sash is compulsory. It is a good plan to take a sash, or long cotton or silk scarf from home, or buy a *sarong* locally. The alternative is to pay for a sash outside each temple.

Dogs

Precisely who owns the obnoxious local dogs is uncertain. No one seems to take any care or responsibility for dogs in Bali. Irritable, dirty and diseased, they go a long way to spoiling an island holiday. Even if you like dogs, you will find

Balinese dogs *ghastly*. Sleep is often ruined by packs of dogs barking at each other across the rice fields. When they howl, the Balinese say they are talking to their ancestors, and do nothing to stop them. Throwing stones, the room vase or your suitcase at them is bad form. *Cicings* (a strong Balinese word for disgusting curs) are especially vile around Mas-Ubud, Semawang and on Nusa Penida. Grit your teeth and take ear-plugs.

PERSONAL PRIORITIES

The Female Traveller
Older, experienced women travellers will probably enjoy a holiday in Jakarta and Bali. But as a lone woman, particularly if using public transport, you should be especially alert. Only experience can avoid some situations. If driving in Bali, a little mechanical knowledge is useful.

Younger women should not become over-friendly with strangers. Play it cool, dress discreetly, and act in a manner that warrants respect. Young female tourists have a bad reputation in Kuta-Sanur due to the behaviour of some Australian girls. An invitation from one Balinese 'beach-boy' is likely to involve his friends. Use a reliable taxi service to commute after dark. It is advisable to spend more, rather than less, on accommodation. Cheap *losmen* attract 'camp-followers'. A little Indonesian may be useful: *saya senag sendiri* means 'I like to be alone', *pergi* means 'go away!'

Babies
Up-market hotels and *losmen* can arrange baby-sitters, although taking a young baby is tough on mother and infant unless you stay in a good, air-conditioned hotel. Diapers are sold in Jakarta department stores and also in Kuta and Sanur. If a child is old enough, a backpack carrier is invaluable.

Venereal Diseases
Jakarta has its share of common venereal diseases, but nothing like Manila, or Bangkok. So far it is missing the AIDS epidemic – isolated cases in Bali have been foreigners. If you think you have caught something, have a lab-test done at the nearest public hospital.

What to Wear
Lightweight cotton trousers and shirts, skirts and blouses, and sportswear are best in the tropical climate of Bali and Jakarta. Dress is very casual on Bali where shorts are acceptable anywhere except temples (see page 103). You will need a warm sweater and waterproof jacket for the mountains and good shoes if you plan climbing the volcanoes. Jakarta is more 'dressed up'. Casual wear is okay in moderately priced hotels, but guests dress at night in better establishments. Waterproof clothing and an umbrella are essential during the monsoon season.

CHILDREN

Most areas in Indonesia are unsuited to family holidays, but Bali and Jakarta are recommended. Balinese love children and children find Bali a fantasy-land. For short stays, Jakarta has recreational parks, zoos and other entertainment. Pulau Seribu islands are ideal for an outdoor family holiday. The many colourful dance and puppet theatre performances on Bali make wonderful entertainment for children of all ages. And of course the beaches will keep a small child happy all day. However, a word of warning: do not leave your child playing with Balinese children; splashing in the shallows, they can attract in a toddler who cannot swim.

TIGHT BUDGET

You can exist for as little as Rp 15,000 (£10.50 or $16) a day (accommodation/meals/drinks) in Bali. This rises to Rp 40,000 (£28 or $42) in Jakarta. For a mere Rp 500 (35p or ¢50) you have a choice of: 10 fried bananas from a street stall; four oranges; a packet (12) of local cigarettes; an airmail stamp for Europe; the English language newspaper; or a shoe-shine (with change).
If your cash is limited, you should perhaps think of visiting Bali in the low season (January to May) when hotel tariffs are reduced – sometimes by as much as 50 per cent. In any case, a homestay or *losmen* provides cheap, and often quite comfortable, lodging. Jakarta is expensive, but some cheaper rooms are available if you are here in time to snap them up. See page 29 for some recommended cheaper hotels.

Market restaurants are a cost-cutting option for meals

Eating can be inexpensive and tasty if you patronise the street stalls that abound in the towns. *Warung* are night foodstalls, open from twilight to about midnight and serving delicious authentic Indonesian food. Remember, however, that *Ramadan* in Muslim Jakarta is not a good time for finding cheap food – expensive Chinese restaurants may be the only places serving meals.

SPECIAL EVENTS

Islamic holidays dominate the religious calendar in Indonesia where 87 per cent of people are Muslims, but every ethnic and religious group – Chinese, Balinese, Christian – celebrates its own festivals. The result is a confusing calendar of events where virtually every day is a nominal holiday.

Jakarta

The Javanese calendar is based on the lunar year (354 days), and varies by about 11 days from year to year. Some of the major Islamic holidays may cause travel inconvenience. *Ramadan* – the fast month – is best avoided in any Muslim country, and during the two-day festival of *Hari Raya* as many as 80 million Javanese are using public transport.

Lebaran, or *Hari Raya*, occurs on the first day of the tenth month after *Ramadan*. Mass prayers are said in mosques and people wear new clothes and exchange presents and food. Like Christmas, St Valentine's Day and New Year rolled in one, *lebaran* celebrations may last a week. Everything is closed on the first two days of *lebaran* in Jakarta. The other major Islamic holiday, *Grebeg Besar*, occurs on the 10th day of the eleventh lunar month, after the annual pilgrimage to Mecca. It is marked by sacrifices when your hotel may slaughter a sheep or goat in the garden for its staff. Meat is distributed to the needy.

Bali

Nyepi is the Balinese 'New Year'. It falls on the spring equinox, and on this day no fire may be lit, no activity carried on and all transport stops. Huge offerings are laid on the crossroads to appease the evil spirits. That night everyone goes out banging gongs, blowing whistles and making as much noise as possible to scare off malevolent spirits for another year.

Temples play an important part in Balinese life, and special occasions are marked with elaborate offerings

Galungan is held annually when the supreme god, Ida Sanghyang Widhi Wasa is believed to descend to earth. Sacrifices of pigs, chickens and ducks are made in his honour. Long, decorated bamboo poles, *(penjors)* are erected outside each house in gratitude for prosperity. During the 10-day festival, *barongs* are taken out of the temples and prance from village to village. On the final day, known as *Kuningan*, when Sanghyang Widhi and other deities depart, offerings are made in their honour. Notable temples where *Galungan* and *Kuningan* ceremonies can be

seen are at: Mengwi, Ulu Watu, Tanah Lot, Goa Lawah and Serangan.

Other Holidays

Kartini Day, 21 April, is a national holiday, commemorating the birthday of Ajeng Kartini (1870-1903), a pioneer in the struggle for the emancipation of Indonesian women. Women wear their national dress on this day.

Proklomasi Kemerdekaan (Independence Day), 17 August, is Indonesian National Independence Day, marked by different celebrations throughout the archipelago.

Armed Forces Day, 5 October, is a public holiday when military parades and army, navy and airforce demonstrations are staged in Jakarta.

SPORT

Popular Pastimes

Cockfighting

Cockfights are illegal, but Balinese take no notice. Banning horse racing would amount to the same thing in England or America. Until it fights, a cock leads a life of luxury. It is fed on a special diet, its feathers are preened and its muscles massaged by an adoring owner. A pet as well as a potential means of income, the bird is carried lovingly wherever its owner goes. You will see men sitting under the village banyan-tree with their cocks. They are taken to *warung* and to village meetings. When the owner goes to the fields, his bird is placed in a bell-shaped bamboo cage, which is stood with others on the roadside for company. With the melodious *gamelan*, the sound of crowing cocks is unmistakable Bali. Cockfights are usually held on the occasion of a temple festival. A group of men – women are not present – gathers outside the gate. Handlers hold the birds aloft for appraisal. Boys rush about collecting bets; sometimes a village may wager a million *rupiah* on a popular fighting cock. When everything is ready, the fight is blessed. The cock's feathers are ruffled and his tail is pulled, but being naturally aggressive the two birds attack. Each rakes the other with razor-spurs tied on to its legs. Dust and feathers fly. Most cockfights are over within 15 seconds with one bird lying mortally injured. Occasionally it is revived by a 'kiss of life' and the audience becomes hysterical as the fight goes on.

Kite-Flying

Balinese adore kite-flying. Graceful kites are believed to please Rare Angon, the shepherd god. Kites are huge, often 26 feet (8m) long, needing a dozen men to launch. The strange 'whoop-whoop-whoop' noise made by the kites is familiar over Sanur and Serangan, where they actually pose a threat to aircraft. *Garuda* and other bird-shaped kites are attractive souvenirs. Villages compete against each other, and the pastime has even become international here now. The biennial international kite-flying contest is held between Sanur and Tohpati in July, August or September.

Bullock-racing

Bullock-races are held after the harvest season in Singaraja and Negara. (See pages 59 and 67). The programme is attended by thousands of farm-workers and their families. The bullocks are given several weeks' practice before the event. Two race together in a Roman-style chariot. Bets are wagered on the animals which, despite their bulk, can run surprisingly fast.

Activities for Visitors

Watersports

Surfing is one of the big attractions of Bali. Kuta-Legian's conditions are good for the less experienced surfer. The experts go to Ulu Watu, and the super-confident tackle the shallow reef-break at Padang Padang, just to the north of there.

Snorkelling. Many of Bali's coastal hotels provide equipment. The best reefs are off Sanur, Candi Dasa and Lovina.

Scuba Diving. The best diving sites are away from the busy tourist areas and require a boat trip to get there. There are clubs offering excursions to the best areas.

Waterskiing is avilable from Sanur, Kuta, Nusa Dua and Benoa on the coast and, best of all, on Lake Bratan in Central Bali.

Sailing and Windsurfing. Sailing in a native *prahu* is an exciting experience. You go out in one of these outrigger fishing boats with the owner.

More conventional sailing is available at watersports clubs in Kuta, Sanur, Nusa Dua and Benoa. **Windsurfing** equipment can also be hired here.

Golf

On Bali there is a splendid golf course above Lake Bratan at the Bali Handara Country Club. The Bali Hyatt and Bali Beach hotels in Sanur have modest courses.

Tennis

Some of the larger hotels have tennis courts available to non-residents as well as guests. It is advisable to take your own tennis balls.

Climbing

Some of the volcanoes in Central Bali provide a good day's climb (see pages 42 and 51), but there is little to interest the serious climber.

For sports opportunities in Jakarta see page 36.

DIRECTORY

Contents

Arriving
Camping
Crime
Customs
  Regulations
Cycling
Driving
Drugs
Electricity
Embassies and
  Consulates

Emergency
  Telephone
  Numbers
Entertainment
  Information
Health
Holidays, public
Money Matters
Opening Times
Personal Safety
Pharmacists
Photography
Places of Worship

Post Office
Public Transport
Senior Citizens
Student and Youth
  Travel
Telephones
Time
Tipping
Toilets and Washing
  Facilities
Tourist Offices
Travel Agencies

Arriving

The national airline, Garuda
Indonesia, operates daily from
European and North American
airports to Jakarta with onward
connections to Bali. There are
direct flights to Bali from
Australia and New Zealand and
also a few from Europe. It is
difficult to confirm bookings,
and delays are not uncommon;
the flight from London Gatwick
to Soekarno Hatta Airport,
Jakarta, should take 17 hours.
The Dutch airline KLM flies six
times weekly to Jakarta and Bali
from Amsterdam; UTA also has
a regular service from Paris.
Both have connecting flights
from London. Saudia, weekly
outward via Jeddah, is good
value. Shop around for the
cheapest ticket. Book in
advance of Christmas holidays
and the June-September period.

Immigration

Immigration officials are
courteous and efficient, but you
will be sent home if your

Waves lap against the dark sands of Ujung's black beach

passport is not valid for six months from arrival date. Proof of onward-return journey is required. Citizens of UK and European Community countries, Australia, New Zealand, United States and Canada do not require a visa for a stay of up to two months if they are visiting as tourists, staying in hotel-type accommodation. This period cannot be extended without a visa. Others must obtain a tourist visa to 30 days from an Indonesian embassy, or consulate. Two photographs are required. All visitors should acquire a *social visa* if visiting relatives or friends or a *business visa*, if on business. Visa arrangements may alter suddenly, so check before you depart.

Airports
Many visitors will arrive at **Soekarno-Hatta International Airport**, 14 miles (23km) west of Jakarta at Tangerang (tel: 5505001/2). Facilities include bank (open 24 hours); telephones (collect and credit card); trolleys and porters; duty free (expensive and limited); first aid medical facilities (open 24 hours, vaccinations available); tourist information (also offering a hotel reservation service); left luggage (available 24 hours).
Clean WCs, but uncomfortable departure lounges. A new airport will open in the early 1990s.
For flight information, call 5505307/8/9. Note that check-in time is two hours before departure. An international airport departure tax is payable,

on both international and domestic flights. At time of writing, the airport tax on international flights is Rp11,000. Airport buses run every 30 minutes to points in the city where there are taxi connections. Your journey into central Jakarta should take 45 minutes, but rain and traffic jams often extend it to 60 minutes. Some hotels provide a bus. Do not be tricked into taking an air-conditioned limousine unless you want to, as it will cost you a lot more than twice as much as a taxi and many times the bus fare (use 'Blue Bird' or 'President' taxis only). Buses leave Jakarta, to return to the airport, from Gambir railway station and Rawamangun and Blok M bus stations.

On Bali, **Denpasar (Ngurah Rai) International Airport** is eight miles (13km) south of Denpasar; 15 minutes' drive from the city, 20 minutes from Sanur, 15 minutes from Kuta and about an hour from Ubud. Banking facilities are open for all flights. The airport has a hotel bookings desk. Most major hotels have meeting services for arriving guests. Public buses to the city run every five minutes, except between about 02.00-04.00 hrs. Taxis are also available; insist the driver uses his meter. Return to the airport by bus is from Tegal bus station, Jalan Imam Bonjal.
On departure, check in early. The departure lounge is cramped and there is a poor restaurant/bar and duty-free. Airport departure tax is payable as for Jakarta.

You can forget the jet-age and travel by pony-trap in Denpasar

Camping
There are no camping-grounds on Bali, as *losmen*/homestays are within every budget. If you really want to 'rough it', then you could: your equipment may be safe, and then again, it may not.

Chemist see Pharmacists

Crime
Sadly, reporting theft has little result in either Jakarta or Bali. Of Jakarta it is said that if you have two sheep and report one stolen to the police, you will find the other gone when you return.

Jakarta
Jakarta has a bad reputation for pickpockets. Areas frequented by tourists are especially vulnerable. Be extra careful around Blok M, and Pasar Baru near the Hotel Melati. A notorious area for robbery is outside Sarinah Department Store; the bus stop here on Jalan MH Thamrin is a major hit-place despite a police office not far away.
If you report a crime, the

procedure may take hours. Virtually no police speak English.

Bali
Robbery is common on Bali, but, conscious of the island's reputation as a tourist resort, police are cracking down. Armed gangs preying on country travellers have been caught, but certain districts remain risky. (See **Personal Safety** page 118). The worst thieving occurs in Kuta-Legian, but tourists must take some blame. Flaunting valuables, many Australians then complain they were robbed. Often their passport and travellers' cheques disappear from 'under the pillow' when they are drunk. It should be said that crime in Bali, so far only robbery, is not committed by Balinese but by locals from elsewhere in the Indonesian archipelago, and that robbery with violence is rare.

Customs Regulations
The following items, per adult, may be taken duty-free into Indonesia:

For a **one-week** stay: 200 cigarettes or 50 cigars or 100 grams of tobacco. For a **two-week** stay: 400 cigarettes or 100 cigars or 200 grams of tobacco. For a stay **over two-weeks:** 600 cigarettes or 150 cigars or 300 grams of tobacco; up to 2 litres of alcohol (opened); a reasonable amount of perfume; plus gifts up to a value of US$100, or equivalent. Cameras, televisions, radios, cassette and video recorders, computers and typewriters should be declared on arrival. Prohibited items include weapons, ammunition, narcotics and pornography. You may not import, or export, more than Rp 50,000. There are no restrictions on foreign currency.

Cycling

Cycling is an ideal way of sightseeing on Bali. The 125-mile (200km) circle-island tour via the coast is recommended. Generally, minor roads are quiet, but beware of large pot-holes and some steep hills. To cope with hills, put your bike on a *bemo* (see page 121). There are plenty of rent-a-bicycle shops in Kuta-Sanur-Ubud. Finding one that works is a problem. Rent for a day to test whether it can manage a longer journey; then bargain as if your life depends on it (which it does). In particular, check the front and rear brake blocks. See that the bell works to let people, poultry and pigs know you are coming. Dogs are a nuisance. Carry a minimum of gear. Except on the less developed west coast, most towns with reasonable *losmen*

are within a day's easy ride. Repairs are not expensive. Wear a hat and cover exposed arms and legs with sunblock.

Driving

In Jakarta

No foreigner tackles self-drive in Jakarta. Hertz and Avis operate chauffeur-driven limousines (Hertz: tel: 332610/ 332739; Avis: tel: 331974/332900).

On Bali

What Bali earns from tourism does not equate with central government spending on roads. There is a two-lane motorway between Denpasar and Benoa. Elsewhere, roads are badly pot-holed and secondary roads may be tracks. Any sort of self-drive requires considerable skill. Experience of driving in Asia is useful. Denpasar is best avoided: the narrow streets are choked with buses, cars and motorbikes. If you stay somewhere such as Kuta or Candi Dasa, renting a bicycle is recommended (see **Cycling**). Rent a Suzuki, for longer trips away from base.

Self-drive is ideal for three to four companions. Even if you are on your own, it is remarkably cheap. You require an **international driving licence** (available from major motoring organisations in your own country). Driving is on the right. Pull well over for the long distance Denpasar – Jakarta buses, which are recklessly driven. Avoid as far as possible the Denpasar – Gianyar – Klungkung road at peak times. The amount of traffic unfortunately makes any time seem like rush-hour in Bali. Only on the rough, rural roads can you relax.

Roads are well signposted. **Petrol** stations on the other hand are few and far between. When you see one, fill your tank. You can see Bali easily in a week's self-drive. Chauffeurs are available from most rent-a-car companies. **Car rental** on Bali really means jeep-rental. The most popular vehicles for hire are Suzuki, Jimmy and open-top VW safari. The Suzuki is ideal. Shopping around for a good deal is dubious and it is better to pay more to get a reliable car. There are numerous car-rental agencies in Kuta and Denpasar and in Sanur and Ubud, but your hotel should be able to make arrangements for you. **Sindhu Merta,** Jalan Tanjung Sari 30, Sanur, gives good service and has competitive rates (tel: 88354 – English speaking).

Motorcycles. There are frightful motorcycle accidents in Bali. Bad roads are mainly to blame. Although it is hot, wear long trousers in case you skid and suffer 'gravel rash'. Pack mercurochrome or other astringent, and equip yourself for cool, wet weather in the mountains.

Most bikes range between 90 and 125cc. You do not need anything faster. If you do not have an international driving licence, endorsed for a motorcycle, you will need a temporary motorcycle licence valid for one month for Bali. Arranged by the bike's owner, this means a trip to Denpasar. Allow four to five hours to be

A flying masterpiece: kites can be works of art as well as great fun

photographed and fingerprinted, to pass a simple written exam and take a riding test.

Rental charges vary according to the bike, the owner and how long you want it. Shop around. Everyone in Kuta seems to have a bike for hire. Check it thoroughly, and be prepared to pay for something decent. Girls who wish to see Bali on a motorbike can hire a driver for a couple of thousand *rupiah* extra. It also saves paying compulsory insurance.

Punctures are a common occurrence; fortunately you will rarely be far from someone who can fix it for you (look for signs saying 'Presban', 'Servis' or 'Bengkel').

Drugs

Indonesia does not have a serious local drug problem. The fate of foreigners found in possession of drugs varies from immediate deportation to authorities in their country of origin to a jail sentence. Indonesian law requires you to report drug offenders, or face arrest yourself. Without cash, you may remain inside some time. Several foreigners languish in the ill-reputed Kerobokan Prison in Legian on Bali.

Electricity

Most hotels use 220 volts 50 cycles, though some hotels and *losmen* in outlying districts may use 110 volts. Electrical appliances without dual voltage may require a voltage transformer. Sockets accept two-round-pronged plugs. For most Western visitors, an electrical adaptor is needed.

Embassies and Consulates

Embassies
Australia: Jalan MH Thamrin 15, Jakarta (tel: 323109)
Canada: Metropolitan Building 1, 5th floor, Jalan Jendral Sudirman 29, Jakarta (tel: 510709)
Great Britain: Jalan MH Thamrin 75, Jakarta (tel: 330904)

New Zealand: Jalan Diponegoro 41, Jakarta (tel: 330680)
US: Jalan Merdeka Selatan 5, Jakarta (tel: 360360)

Consulates and Foreign Representatives on Bali
There is no British consulate on Bali, but the Australian Consulate handles the affairs of British citizens, plus those of Canadians and New Zealanders.
Australian Consulate, Jalan Raya Sanur 146, Tanjung Bungkak, Denpasar (tel: 25997/8)
Consular Agency of the United States of America, Jalan Segara Ayu 5, Sanur (tel: 88478). Open 08.00-14.00 hrs Monday to Friday, but a consular representative is available 24 hours for emergencies.

Emergency Telephone Numbers
Police 110
Fire 113
Ambulance 118

Jakarta City Health Service 119

Balinese artistry is everywhere

Jakarta Hospitals
RS Aini, Jalan HR Rasuna Said Kuningan (tel: 516109)
RS Auri, Jalan Kesehatan IV/26 (tel: 342940)
RS Unika Atmajaya, Jalan Pluit Raya 2 (tel: 661909)

Bali Police
Jalan Diponegoro, Denpasar (tel: 110)
Jalan Ray Kuta, Kuta (tel: 51598)

Bali Hospitals/Clinics
Sanglah Public Hospital, Jalan Kesehatan 1, Sanglah Denpasar (tel: (0361) 27911)
Wangaya Public Hospital, Jalan Kartini, Denpasar (tel: 22141)
Army Hospital, Jalan Sudirman, Denpasar (tel: 28003)
Dharma Usaha Clinic, Jalan Sudirman 50, Denpasar (tel: 27560)
Manuaba Clinic, Jalan HOS, Cokroaminoto 28, Denpasar (tel: 26393)
Psychiatric Clinic, Dr I Gst Putu Panteri, Jalan Raya Denpasar, Tabanan (tel: 25744)
Emergency Dental Treatment, Dr Indra Guizot, Jalan Pattimura 19, Denpasar (tel: 22445, 26445)
Surya Husadha Clinic, Jalan Pulau Serangan 1-3, Denpasar (tel: 25249). This private hospital is specially geared to tourists. It offers insurance cover for your stay on the island.

Entertainment Information
For current information on entertainment in Jakarta, consult the *Jakarta Post's* 'What's On' section or *Guide to Jakarta* tourist magazine (free in travel agencies and hotels). The English-language paper *Indonesian Times* has a 'Where To Go' section (also for Bali).

Health
No health regulations apply in Indonesia, except inoculation against yellow fever if coming from an infected zone.
Visiting Jakarta and Bali can be medically safe if you take precautions. This applies mainly to what you eat and drink and how much you expose yourself to sun. Take it easy for 48 hours after you arrive. Jet-lag changes your sleeping and eating patterns and your body is most vulnerable to climatic changes at this time. No special medications are required; both Jakarta and Bali are malaria free, but you are advised to take the precaution of having a tetanus injection. Mosquitoes are a menace, so equip yourself with a good repellent. Most non-air-conditioned hotels supply coils, or spray your room. Adhere to the following basic rules and you will, with luck, remain healthy.
Wear a hat, sunglasses and high protection sunscreen (Factor 15+).
If you sweat profusely, you may need to **take salt-tablets.**
Drink plenty. Local water is unsafe, but good, cheap bottled water is sold everywhere. If you cannot obtain any, drink fresh coconut juice. Local beer is a good thirst-quencher in the tropics.
Do not over-indulge. Drinking plus eating plus sun often equals upset stomach. Usually non-infectious, diarrhoea often results from this combination, or from eating hot, unfamiliar, spicy dishes. Plain boiled rice, or *bubur* (rice cooked in stock with vegetables) is

Herbal medicine on sale in the Sarinah Department Store, Jakarta

recommended while the stomach is recovering. Carry anti-diarrhoeal tablets and avoid ice cubes. Most hotels know the dangers of contaminated water and supply jugs of boiled water, but drop a water-purifying tablet in to be sure.

Gastro-intestinal diseases can be picked up anywhere, but they are less likely to be encountered in a de luxe hotel, a *warung* where locals eat, or Chinese restaurants where food is freshly prepared.

Second-grade hotels with sub-standard cooking and hygiene arrangements are often suspect. Food cooked in the streets – bananas, sweet potato, etc – is generally safe. Check the cooking oil is clean and buy only freshly cooked food, not from a ready-cooked pile. Except in specialised food outlets, eating yoghurt or ice-cream is risky.

Doctors (Doktor)

Ask your hotel (if staying in a cheap *losmen*, contact an international hotel and ask the concierge) to recommend a doctor, or call your embassy, or the European manager of your airline. A Chinese doctor is preferable. Jakarta has the best medical services. Only a hospital, not a clinic, will take an emergency case. If seriously ill, fly home. Bali has a poor reputation for health services, although there is a special ward for tourists in the main hospital in Denpasar. (See **Emergency Telephone Numbers** page 115 for hospitals.)

Medical Treatments

Jamu are cheap, traditional medicines made from plants, minerals and animals. You can recognise a *jamu* stall by the shelves of little jars and packets Find someone who can translate your problem – the vendor will have precisely what you need... and it may cure you!

Sarinah Department Store in Jakarta has a traditional medicine counter in the basement. If you want something for a cold, flu or a sprain, 'Silver Clove' medicated balm, Balsam Cengkeh 10 is excellent.

See also **Pharmacists**

Take out adequate travel insurance, including a provision to get 'medi-vacced' by air-ambulance if necessary.

Holidays, public

1 January: New Year's Day is observed throughout the country.
21 April: Kartini Day

17 August: Proklomasi Kemerdekaan (Independence Day)
5 October: Armed Forces Day
25 December: Christmas Day
In addition, there are the Muslim religious festivals of *lebaran* and *Grebeg Besar* and the Chinese New Year celebrations (all based on the lunar calendar); the Balinese New Year (Nyepi) in March/April; and Good Friday and Ascension Day, celebrated by Christians.
See also **Special Events** pages 105 – 107).

Money Matters

The Indonesian unit of currency is the *rupiah*, which comes in the following denominations: bill/banknotes: Rp100, Rp500, Rp1,000, Rp5,000, Rp10,000 coins: Rp5, Rp10, Rp25, Rp50, Rp100
It is a good plan to have sufficient *rupiah* in smaller denominations (Rp50, Rp100), as many taxi drivers and small stores may not have small change. It is also advisable to take enough *rupiah* when travelling outside major tourist destinations. Daily exchange rates are posted at banks and in leading daily newspapers. In Indonesia, money-changers give a better rate than hotels. Banks in Jakarta give a better rate of exchange than in outlying areas. Shop around. Travellers' cheques can usually be cashed at hotels, banks and money-changers.
Credit cards are widely accepted in Jakarta and popular tourist resorts in Bali. Use Visa, Diners Club and American Express for preference.
Banking hours are from 07.30./08.00 to 12.30/13.00 hrs (and for a time in the afternoon), Mondays to Fridays; and from 08.00 to 12.00/13.00 hrs on Saturdays. Cash desks in banks may not be open in the afternoons and will also close at least one hour before the bank closes.

Opening Times

Government offices in Indonesia generally open from 08.00 to 15.00 hrs from Monday to Thursday; from 08.00 to 11.30hrs on Friday and from 08.00 to 14.00 hrs on Saturday.
Business offices have varied hours. Some open from 08.00 to 16.00, others from 09.00 to 17.00 hrs. Other offices work half day on Saturdays; some are closed.
Banks open from 07.30 or 08.00 hrs to about 16.00 hrs. Most banks are also open Saturday mornings. Cash desks close at least one hour before the bank closes. Money-changers stay open till evening.
Indonesians like to complete most work before the midday heat. The best time to make appointments is between 08.00 and 11.00 hrs.

On Bali, government offices are open from 08.00 to 14.00 hrs Monday to Thursday, on Fridays until 11.00 hrs, and some Saturdays until 12.30 hrs. Most shops, stores and shopping-centres are open six days a week, from 08.00 to 15.00 hrs and from 17.00 to 20.00 hrs in the evening, except on public holidays. Some shops open on Sundays.

Personal Safety

Crime against the person is rare in Indonesia, but theft is something to guard against. In Jakarta, expect to be robbed if you travel on local buses. Thieves – often from Sumatra – work in gangs. One, perhaps a girl, will distract you with a pleasantry. Once your gaze is averted, the gang will strike. It is unlikely you can react as the culprit melts into the crowd. Never carry your airline ticket, passport or more money than necessary. If shopping, a credit card in a buttoned-up breast pocket is ideal. Be alert. Avoid walking about after dark. Ignore anyone slowing down in a car, or *bejaj* (see page 121). On Bali, the Lake Batur area is crime-prone. Be careful of your bag, camera, pocket. Do not leave a rented vehicle without a companion to guard it. It may not start when you return. Do not engage in conversation in this area. The people are different from on the coast. The Kintamani-Bangli region is dubious, but as with everything, it all depends who is up to no good when you are there. In the coastal resorts, take nothing to the beach unless someone you know can watch it while you swim. Enquire if your hotel, or *losmen* has a security box. The money-changer at 'Bemo Corner' in Kuta has safe-deposit facilities. Be careful of mini-buses, *bemos* and *bejaj* which stop without being hailed. Also, on crowded *bemos* beware of smiling faces offering assistance by taking your luggage and placing it at the far end of the compartment, do not be surprised if your bag feels lighter at the end of the journey. Ideally try to travel with Balinese women and children.

Pharmacists

You can obtain most drugs – analgesics, antibiotics, vitamins, etc – from local pharmacists *(apotiki)*. A prescription is unnecessary. Bargain in smaller pharmacies.

Most medications are expensive, so make up a small kit from home: water purifying tablets, aspirin or other pain-killer, anti-diarrhoeal tablets, vitamin C, lip-balm, Dettol/astringent, first aid dressings, decongestant, etc.

Photography

Indonesia, especially Bali, is one of the most photogenic places on earth. Most people do not object to being photographed but if they do, desist. Anyone connected with the tourist trade may require payment. You should oblige with a small sum if the photo is important. Photography shops in Kuta-Legian and Sanur on Bali develop prints rapidly and usually well. Jalan Agus Salim is where to develop and buy film in Jakarta; also for cameras. Slow speed film is okay for the coast. You will need faster – 100 ASA – in misty mountain areas. A flash is useful, but should not be used when photographing temple ceremonies. Never leave your camera in a bus as the heat will destroy the film. A plastic bag protects your camera in sudden showers. Museums in Jakarta charge for photography (Rp500 for still cameras, Rp1,000 for videos).

The beauty of a Balinese temple pond. Religion dominates life here

Places of Worship

In Jakarta, the **Gereja Immanuel** at Jalan Merdeka Timur has Protestant Sunday services in Dutch and English.
The following Christian services are held on Bali:

Holy Mass
Denpasar: **St Joseph Church, Kepundung** – Saturday, 17.30 hrs. Sunday, 07.00, 08.30 and 17.30 hrs.
Hotel Bali Beach, Sanur, Legong Room – Saturday, 18.00 hrs (in English).
Hotel Bali Hyatt, Sanur: Hibiscus Room – Saturday, 19.00 hrs (in English).
Nusa Dua Beach Hotel: Garuda Room – Sunday, 18.00 hrs (in English).
Hotel Melia Bali Sol, Nusa Dua: Bali Room – Sunday, 18.00 hrs in English).
Kuta: **St Francis Xavier Church** – Saturday, 18.00 hrs. Sunday, 18.00hrs.

Protestant Services
Denpasar: **Maranatha Church, Surapati** – Sunday, 09.00 and 18.00 hrs.
Gereja Kirsten Protestan di Bali, Jalan Debes – Sunday 07.00, 09.00 and 18.00 hrs.
Hotel Bali Beach, Sanur: Legong Room – Sunday, 18.00 hrs (in English).
Hotel Putra Bali, Nusa Dua: Bale Ubud – Sunday, 17.30 hrs (in English).

Police see Crime

Post Office
Most hotels in Jakarta provide postal services. If you prefer to mail your letter, the following are some post addresses:
Central Post Office, Jalan Pos Utara 2, Pasar Baru (tel: 350004)
Gajahmada Post Office, Jalan Gajahmada (tel: 346595)
Jakarta Kota Post Office, Jalan Fatahillah 3 (tel: 679800).

Post Office addresses on Bali are:
Denpasar: **Central Post Office,** Jalan Raya Puputan, Renon
Sanur: Banjar Taman, Sanur
Kuta: Jalan Ray Tuban, Kuta
Ubud: Banjar Taman, Ubud
Singaraja: Jalan Gajahmada, Singaraja
All offer poste restante.

Public Transport

Inter-island Travel
Inter-island travel is effected by regular air services of Garuda Indonesia and its subsidiary Merpati using B737, DC-9, F28 and A300 airbus. Other airlines offering domestic flights are Bouraq, Mandala, Sempati, Seulawah and Zamrud. Scheduled ferry sailings and

irregular departures by *bugis*
schooners make up a
miraculously good overall
communications network.
Addresses in Jakarta of Garuda
Indonesia and other domestic
airlines are:

Garuda Indonesia, BDN
Building, Jalan MH Thamrin 5,
(tel: 334425, 334429, 334430,
334434)
Bouraq Indonesia Airlines, Jalan
Angkasa (tel: 6595194, 6595179)
Mandala Airlines, Jalan Veteran
1/34 (tel: 368107)
Merpati Nusantara Airlines,
Jalan Angkasa 2 (tel: 417404,
413608)
Pelita Air Service, Jalan Abdul
Muis 52-54 (tel: 375908)

Huge pinisis *ply between islands in
the Indonesian archipelago*

Sempati Air Transport, Jalan
Merdeka Timur 7 (tel: 348760,
343323)

Addresses of airline offices on
Bali are:
Garuda Indonesia: Jalan Melati
61, Denpasar (tel: 24550)
Bouraq Indonesia Airlines: Jalan
Sudirman 19A, Denpasar (tel:
24656)
Merpati Nusantara: Jalan Melati
57, Denpasar (tel: 22864/35358).

Visitors can travel from Jakarta
by rail to all the major cities and
towns in Java and to towns in the
southern part of Sumatra via
Merak. For connections with
Bali, the State Railways offer a
combination bus/train ticket
from Bali to Jakarta, but not the
other way around.
Denpasar is the main travel
terminus on Bali. Boat, train and
plane tickets are sold here. For
travel to Jakarta, Lorena
Continental overland bus is
recommended. It has air
conditioning, WC, videos.
Travelling time from Denpasar
to Jakarta is 1½ days. Fare
includes snacks and a lunch.

Getting About Jakarta
Buses: Some 20 bus companies
operate all over Jakarta. They
are cheap, crowded and
difficult to board. If you take a
bus, sit at the front and beware
of pickpockets. **Be alert for
thieves at a bus-stop.** Avoid
Jakarta rush-hour between
07.30-08.30 and 16.00-17.30 hrs.
Mini-buses, or *oplets* (slightly
more expensive) are safer, with
seated passengers only.
Bus Terminals are at Gambir
Railway Station; Jalan Bulungan,

Blok M Kemayoran Baru;
Kemayoran; Rawamangun;
Pasar Minggu; and Halim
Perdana Kusuma.
**See under Arriving for services
to Jakarta's main airport.** There
is also a regular bus shuttle
serving the city's second airport,
Halim Perdana Kusama.
Bejaj: These noisy rattle-traps
are motorised three-wheel taxis,
often the quickest way to
commute. Take a scarf to shield
your face from the fumes as
locals do. Bargain the fare; if
this is disputed by the driver,
wave him on and wait for
another. A chartered *bejaj*
between three companions is a
good plan for sightseeing. Learn
where you wish to go in
Indonesian as the driver will not
speak English. *Bejaj* are found
all over the city.
Taxis: Beware of private taxis.
Avoid yellow cabs. Take only
Bluebird and President.
Bluebird: tel: 325607 (blue)
President: tel: 4895978
(yellow/red).
Taxis have a special hourly rate
for sightseeing trips.

Getting About Bali
Buses: Buses cover the main
'inter-town' routes, with
Denpasar as the central
terminal. In addition, all main
routes, as well as minor
passable ones are covered by
Colts and *bemos* (see below).
Bemos: This is the most popular
means of transport. The Bali
version of the *bejaj,* it is a small,
noisy three-wheel motorbike-
axi, driven recklessly in and out
of traffic-jams. Most operate a
standard route, picking up and
depositing passengers along the

way. *Bemo* drivers have a price
for locals and another price for
tourists. Ask Balinese travellers
what they pay. Beware of
pickpockets on popular tourist
routes such as Kuta-Legian-
Denpasar-Ubud. A fun idea is to
charter a *bemo* for a day, or
longer. Pick a good one.
Regular *bemos* can squeeze in
12 people. Do not get into a
bemo with three, or four
apparently friendly young men.
An unfortunate sign of the times
is that they might rob you. (see
Personal Safety page 118).
There are four main bus and
bemo terminals in Denpasar:
Ubung (serving the west and
north of Bali); Kereneng (the
east); Tegal (services Kuta and
Nusa Dua); and Wangaya (a
route north via Sangeh). Another
small bus station, Suci, serves
points south, including Benoa
Port.
Colts: the name comes from
Mitsubishi Colt mini-buses but
any small bus is known as a
'Colt'. They are marginally more
expensive than a larger bus, but
are more comfortable. They ply
everywhere on Bali.
See also **Cycling** and **Driving.**

Senior Citizens
Indonesia is not suitable for
elderly tourists unless they are
especially fit and able to cope
with the heat. Bali's rough roads
and temple stairways are very
taxing.

Student and Youth Travel
Indonesia is ideal for youth
travel. It offers bargain-priced
adventure. Student-cards are
recognised by many places. Bali
is in particular geared to young
visitors and many may find the

surf, shops and bars of Kuta
ideal.

Telephones

Indonesia's own satellite offers
efficient communications
overseas. Direct dialling is
available in major hotels which
may not charge more than 10
per cent on top of operator
calls. However, it is cheaper in
major cities like Jakarta and
Denpasar to dial from the city
telephone office (Kantor
Telekommunikasi).There are
collect and credit card
telephones in the departure
lounges of Soekarno Hatta and
Denpasar airports.

To telephone to the UK from
Indonesia, dial 0044, then the
local STD code (minus the first
0) and the customer number.
For operator assistance in
making your international call,
dial 101 or, in Jakarta, 104. The
dialling code for Indonesia from
abroad is 01062, plus 21 for
Jakarta and 361 for Denpasar.

Time

Indonesia is divided into three
time zones. Western Indonesia
Standard Time (including
Sumatra, **Java,** West Kalimantan,
Central Kalimantan) is seven
hours ahead of Greenwich
Mean Time (GMT); Central
Indonesia Standard Time (East
Kalimantan, South Kalimantan,
Bali, Sulawesi, Nusatenggara) is
eight hours ahead; and Eastern
Indonesia Standard Time, which
covers Irian Jaya and the
Maluku islands, is nine hours
ahead of GMT.

Thus for most of the year, when
it is 12 noon in Bali it is 04.00 hrs
in London; 23.00 hrs (the
previous day) in New York and

*The stillness of the lakes near
Bedugal, in Bali's Central Mountains*

Montreal; 14.00 hrs in Sydney;
and 16.00 hrs in New Zealand.
When it is 12 noon in Jakarta it is
05.00 hrs in London; 12 midnight
in New York and Montreal;
15.00 hrs in Sydney; and 17.00
hrs in New Zealand.

Tipping

Tipping is not traditional in
Indonesia, but there are certain
charges for services such as
airport porterage. Leading
hotels and restaurants add 10
per cent service to bills. Where
they do not, a 10-15 per cent tip
is now customary. Porters and
others who perform services are
often grateful for a small tip of
Rp 500-1,000. Leave taxi drivers
small change. Do not, however,
insist on giving anyone a tip, as
many Balinese look on tipping
as charity and find it humiliating

Toilets and Washing Facilities

All tourist hotels have western-style WCs. Elsewhere are squat lavatories, flushed by water from a dipper which floats in a tub of water by the toilet, or a tap. Water from the dipper is used by Indonesians to cleanse themselves. It is advisable to carry a supply of paper. A bin is often provided for soiled material, which would block the system. There are next to no public WCs although they are always installed in museums. If you need a lavatory, go into a hotel or café. The better the establishment, the better the WC.

Cheaper hotels and *losmen* have Indonesian-style bathrooms, or *mandi*, with tiled floors and a tub which you fill with water. Do not sit in the tub as you might get stuck. Stand beside it and pour water over yourself with the plastic dipper, or *gajung*. Hot water is rare in cheap establishments; you may miss it in mountain areas. For that reason, take a *mandi* around 17.00 hours, before the evening chill sets in.

Tourist Offices

One of the main reasons why Indonesia is not better known as a tourist destination is the dearth of tourist promotion offices abroad. There is no official government tourist office in London – in fact the only European office is in Frankfurt (see below). Writing direct to Jakarta is useless. For UK travellers, the airline **Garuda Indonesia** has limited numbers of brochures (35 Duke Street, London W1M 5DF, tel: (071) 935 7055). **Indonesian Express Travel Agent:** 70 New Bond Street, London, W1Y 9DE (tel: (071) 491 4469) is a potential source of information, but their main function is to promote their own tours and travel services. The **Indonesian Embassy,** 38 Grosvenor Square, London W1X 9AD (tel: (071) 499 7661), may be able to help with certain enquiries.

Europe
Indonesia Tourist Promotion Offices, Wiessenhutten Strasse, 17, D6000, Frankfurt-am-Main (tel: (0611) 233681).

North America
Indonesia Tourist Promotion Offices, 3457 Wilshire Boulevard, Los Angeles, CA 90010, USA (tel: (213) 3872078).

Australia
Indonesia Tourist Promotion Offices, 4 Bligh Street, PO Box 3836, Sydney 200 (tel: (02) 232 6044).

Tourist Information Offices in Jakarta

Visitor Information Centres
Jakarta Theatre Building, Jalan MH Thamrin 9, Jakarta Pusat 10340 (tel: 354094; 364093)
Oriental Building, Jalan MH Thamrin 51, Jakarta Pusat 10350 (tel: 332067)

Visitor Information Service
Jakarta International Airport, Soekarno-Hatta Cengkareng, Jakarta Barat 19110 (tel: 5507088)

Jakarta Metropolitan City Tourism Development Board
Jalan KH Abdul Rohim 2, Kuningan Barat, Jakarta Selatan 12710 (tel: 511073, 511369, 510738).

DIRECTORY

Oriental grace: the water palace complex of Tirtagangga

Tourist Information Offices on Bali:

Government Tourist Information Building
Jalan Bakunsari, Kuta (tel: 51419)

Bali Government Tourist Office
Jalan Raya Pupatan, Renon, Denpasar (Sanur exit), tel: 22387.

Badung Government Tourist Office (Badung District)
Jalan Surapati 7, Denpasar (near central museum), tel: 23602/23399.
Open: 08.00-14.00 hrs (until 11.00 hrs Friday and 12.30 hrs Saturday). Closed Sunday.
Tourist information offices are also found in Gianyar, Ubud and Singaraja, but they are disappointing.

Travel Agencies
There are countless tour operators offering a variety of tour programmes on Bali. Most agencies are in Denpasar, Kuta-Legian and Sanur.

Compare prices. If you can, check with someone who has done a tour. Some tour programmes pack too much into eight to nine hours' drive – remember Bali's roads are rough and busy.
Major operators include:
BIL (Bali Indonesia Ltd), Jalan Semawang, Sanur
Natrabu, Jalan Seruni 21, Denpasar
Pacto, Jalan Tanjung Sari, Sanur
Examples of tours offered are:
An eight-hour **Kintamani** tour by BIL visiting Lake Batur and stopping in Celuk, Mas, Ubud and Tampaksiring on the way.
A four-hour tour of **Sangeh** and **Mengwi** by Pacto visiting the Royal Temple of Taman Ayun and the Holy Monkey Forest of Sangeh.
A seven-hour tour to **Besakih** by Natrabu stopping in Klungkung and other points along the way. If you make only one tour, visit Mas-Ubud and Bedugal - Lake Bratan.

For travel agencies in Jakarta see page 19.

LANGUAGE

More than 250 languages and dialects are spoken in Indonesia, but the lingua franca is *Bahasa Indonesia*, spoken by the majority. In Jakarta one in ten people also speaks some English. Balinese is altogether different. It has a different vocabulary and conversation is complicated by caste, depending to whom you are speaking (see page 103). Concentrate on *Bahasa Indonesia:* it makes travel easier and people are delighted to be addressed in their own language. *Pasar* or 'market' Indonesian is a simplified, colloquial form. Similar to Malay, *Bahasa Indonesia* has no complex rules, nor the tonal complications that make Asian languages difficult.

Grammar

Indonesian has no articles, genders or cases; conjunctions are likewise unknown. To form the plural, double the noun, eg suitcase – *kopor*, suitcases *kopor kopor*. An adjective is always placed after the noun. To make a question of a sentence, simple raise the pitch of your voice at the end of the phrase. Indonesian is phonetic. Most consonants sound like English consonants. Vowels are more confusing: pronounce 'a' like the 'u' in 'up' – eg *apa kabar* (how are you?); 'e' is a short sound not always pronounced, eg *selamat datang* (welcome) becomes *slamat datang*.

Indonesian is written in Latin characters adapted from an early Arabic version, using 21 letters of the alphabet. Remember that each single letter represents a sound. Below are some useful words and phrases:

Basics

I, my and mine saya
no tidak
yes ya
he, she, it/his, her, its dia
good bagus
you kamu
we (including the person addressed) kita
we (not including the person addressed) kami
they mereka
big besar
small kecil
welcome selamat datang
good morning (until 11.00 hrs) selamat pagi
good afternoon (11.00-15.00 hrs) selamat siang
good afternoon (15.00 hrs to nightfall) selamat sore
good evening selamat malam
good night selamat tidur
enjoy your meal selamat makan
thank you terima kasih
excuse me ma'af permisi
how are you? apa kabar?
goodbye sampai bertemu lagi
what is that? apaka itu?
do you speak English? saudara bicara bahasa Inggris?
I don't understand saya tidak mengerti
I would like saya minta

Directions

where dimana
from dari
to ke
here kemana
there demana
straight ahead terus
stop berhenti
north utara

south selatan
east timur
west barat
left kiri
right kanan
near dekat
far jauh
direction jurusan
down/below bawah
up/above atas

Numbers
1 satu
2 dua
3 tiga
4 empat
5 lima
6 enam
7 tujuh
8 delapan
9 sembilan
10 sepuluh
11 sebelas
12 duabelas
13 tigabelas
20 dua puluh
30 tiga puluh
100 seratus
1000 seribu
2000 duaribu
10,000 sepuluh ribu
100,000 seratus ribu
500,000 lima ratus
1 million satu juta

Food
Makan is both the verb 'to eat' and the noun 'food'. A restaurant is therefore *rumah makan*, or 'house food'. Below are some basic items of food and drink:
bread roti
sweets gula-gula
egg telur
chilli lombok
ginger jahe
salt garam
pepper merika
sugar gula
fish ikan

oysters tiram
crab kepiting
prawn udang
shrimp udang kecil

Vegetables
cucumber mentimun
beans buncis
onion bawang
potato kentang

Drinks
beer bir
boiled water air putih
orange/lemon juice air jeruk/air jeruk nipis
coffee kopi
milk susu
rice wine brem
tea teh
May we have our bill please?
Coba berikan rekening saya?

In the Restaurant
The following words will help you to read the menu:
nasi putih plain white rice
nasi goreng fried rice with ancillaries such as fried egg, chicken, peppers etc, but usually meaning fried rice
nasi sayur rice with vegetables
nasi campur rice with a selection of things including meat
nasi padang rice with spicy side-dishes.
mie kuah noodle soup
babi guling roast baby pig
betutu bebek steamed duck
gado-gado cold cooked vegetable salad (lettuce, cucumber, tomato, hard-boiled egg, etc) with peanut sauce
saté chicken or lamb barbecued on skewers and eaten with peanut dip
cap cai vegetable or meat chop suey
rijstaffel a selection of Indonesian dishes of Dutch colonial tradition

accommodation (see also local details) 93-4
Agung Karangasem 37, 38
air travel 109, 110, 119-20
Amlapura 38-9
Ancol Dreamland 22

babies and children 104-5
Bali
 history 11
 maps 38-9, 46-7
 places to visit 37-76
 wildlife and countryside 9-10, 77-86
Bali Barat National Park 78-9
Bali Museum 47
Bangli 40
banks 117
Batubulan 40
Beautiful Indonesia in Miniature 24-6
Bedugul 40-1
Benoa 42
Besakih 42
Blahbatuh 43
Bona 43
budget tips 105
Bukit Jamba 43
buses 110, 120-1

camping 111
Candi Dasa 43-5
Canggu 45
car rental 113
Celuk 45
chemists 118
Cibodas National Park 79-80
climate 100-1
cockfighting 107-8
Culik 46
culture and entertainment (see also local details) 94-100, 115
currency 117
customs regulations 111-12
cycling 112

Denpasar 46-9
dress 104
driving 112-13

eating out see local details
embassies and consulates 114
emergencies 114

festivals and events 105-7
Fine Arts Museum (Museum Seni Rupa), Jakarta 23
food and drink 87-90
forests 82-4

Gianyar 49
Gilimanuk 49-50
Gitgit 50
Glodok 19
Goa Gajah 50
Goa Lawah 50
Gunung Agung 42-3
Gunung Batur 50-1
Gunung Kawi 52

health matters 115-16

Indonesia 4-8
Indonesia Museum 25
inoculation 115
Istiqlal Mosque 19

Jakarta 17-36
 accommodation 27-9
 eating out 30-4
 map 16-17
 nightlife and entertainment 29-30
 shopping 34-6
 sightseeing 18-27
 sports facilities 36
Jakarta City Museum (Museum Fatahillah) 23
Jatiluwih 52
Java, wildlife and countryside 79-86

Kamasan Village 54
Kintamani 52-3
Klungkung 53-4

Komodo dragons 86
Krambitan 54
Kusamba 54
Kuta 54-7

Lake Batur 50-1
language 125-6
Legian 57-8
local etiquette 103
local time 122
Lovina 58
Lubang Buaya 26

mangrove swamps 86
maps
 Bali 38-9, 46-7
 Bali and Java – Wildlife 80-1
 Indonesia 8-9
 Jakarta 16-17
 Ubud 73
Mas 59
Medan Merdeka, Jakarta 20
medical treatment 115, 116
Mengwi 59
money 117
motorcycle rental 113
Museum Bahari, Jakarta 22
Museum Neka, Ubud 73
Museum Puri Lukisan, Ubud 72-3
music and dance 94-8

National Monument (Monumen Nasional) 20
National Museum, Jakarta (Museum Pusat) 23
national parks and reserves 78-82
Negara 59
nightlife see local details
Nusa Dua 60
Nusa Lembongan 10, 60, 61
Nusa Penida 60-1

opening hours 117
orchid gardens 21

INDEX

Pacung 62
Padangbai 62
Pasar Ikan 20-1
passports and visas 109-10
Pejeng 62-3
Pelangi 26-7
Peliatan 63
Penelokan 63-4
personal safety 104, 111, 118
photography 118
places of worship 119
post offices 119
public holidays 116-17
public transport 119-21
Pulaki 64
Pulau Seribu 26-7
Puppet Museum (Museum Wayang), Jakarta 24
Pura Gaduh 43
Pura Kehen 40
Pura Penataran Sasih 62
Putri 27

Ragunan Zoo (Kebun Binatang Ragunan) 26
rail travel 120
religion 7, 12-13

Sangeh 64
Sanur 64-7
Seba 27
Semawang 65
senior citizens 121
Serangan Island 67
shopping (see also local details) 90-2
Singaraja 67-8
social customs 14-15, 101-3
sports and leisure activities (see also local details) 108
student and youth travel 121-2
Sukawati 68

Tabanan 68-9
Taman Anggrek Gelora Senayan 21
Taman Budaya, Denpasar 47
Taman Fatahillah, Jakarta 21-2
Taman Impian Jaya Ancol 22
Taman Mini Indonesia 24-6
Tampaksiring 69
Tanah Lot 69
taxis 110, 121

telephones 122
temples 12-13
Tenganan 69-70
Textile Museum (Museum Tekstil), Jakarta 24
Thousand Islands 26-7
tipping 122
Tirtagangga 70
toilets 123
tourist information 123-4
Toya Bungkah 51
travel agencies 124
Trunyan 71
Tulamben 71-2

Ubud 72-5
   map 73
Ujung 76, 109
Ujung Kulon National Park 80-1
Ulu Watu 76

voltage 114

wildlife 78-9, 80, 81-2, 84, 85-6
words and phrases 125-6

Yeh Sanih 76

The Automobile Association would like to thank the following photographers and libraries for their assistance in the preparation of this book.

CHRISTINE OSBORNE took all the photographs in this book except those listed below (© AA Photo Library).

NATURE PHOTOGRAPHERS LTD 78 Lar gibbon, 79 Leaf insect (S C Bisserot), 80 Black drongo (M Hill), 83 Tree ferns (K J Carlson), 84 Atlas beetle, 84 Blue-tailed banded pitta (S C Bisserot).

SPECTRUM COLOUR LIBRARY Cover Traditional Dance.

Author's Acknowledgements
The author thanks the following for their assistance with this book: **Jakarta** – Beranti Ismail (Jakarta Hilton), Annie Latifah (Sabang Hotel), Tjhan Matius (Apexindo Tours), Abeng Arbella (Cruise Division, Bil Tours). **Bali** – Wayan Putra Pata (Bali Government Tourist Office), Tangkas Surapta (Badung Tourism Office), Made Patera (Puri Buitan Hotel), Desak Ketut Murni (Semawang Hotel).